...And So We PRAY 2

Dearst Mindy, Trust i
Our lord who lovs MC
more tha you knowl(and
more than you do!)

Maulectt Hayon

... *And So We*
PRAY 2

SUPPORTING YOUNG ADULTS THROUGH THE COLLEGE YEARS

Maribeth Harper

Mindy
_7036230603_

CONTENTS

DEDICATION

*This book was inspired by Praying College Moms, a ministry
of women who gather in their parishes to support one another
and pray for their college-age young adults. The group places
all college-age children, their families, and all who care for
them under the protective mantle of the
Blessed Mother Mary, Our Lady of the Rosary.*

ABOUT...*AND SO WE PRAY 2*

...*And So We Pray 2* is the second book in a series that accompanies mothers as they send their children off to college. Each book is filled with encouragement, sound Catholic teaching, and real-life stories shared by women of faith who have experienced the transition from active family life to empty nesting and everything in between. The books may be read in any order, as each book stands alone.

As mothers, we want to activate the most powerful weapon imaginable to help our children succeed in their college-aged years. That weapon is prayer. ...*And So We Pray* and ...*And So We Pray 2* will help you pray by providing you with thought-provoking, faith-based, real-life applications to contemporary issues you and your young adult may face during the exciting and sometimes challenging college years.

ACKNOWLEDGMENTS

MANY THANKS TO the mothers and young adults who shared with me their hearts and their stories for the edification and blessing of others. Thanks also to the dedicated women of Praying College Moms, especially to the founder, Laurel Howanitz, and Liz Hild, Anita Alexander, Julie Mantooth, and Frances Chamberlin, for their support, encouragement, and example. I am also grateful for Fr. John Pietropaoli, LC, and Fr. Justin Huber of the Archdiocese of Washington, D.C., who read the book for doctrinal soundness and offered their wise advice. I thank Melissa Overmyer who generously created an excellent training video for small-group leaders that can be accessed on prayingcollegemoms.org. Finally, I thank my daughter, Sarah Nolan,—my first reader of every chapter—and my husband, Denis, of thirty-three years for their patience and loving oversight.

HOW TO USE THIS BOOK

...AND SO WE PRAY 2 and the original, *...And So We Pray*, were written for individuals or for women meeting in small groups who want to explore issues that young adults face in the college-aged years and read, discuss, and/ or pray about how faith in Jesus Christ can console and strengthen us.

Each chapter includes the following elements:

- The body of the chapter, which focuses on a dilemma and proposes a principle of faith as a possible solution.
- The closing prayer.
- Questions for Reflection—these can be used individually or in small-group settings.
- Prayer Intentions—a place for writing down prayers of petition.
- Answered Prayers—a place for recognizing and celebrating answered prayers, which help to build faith and trust in God.

- Prayer Practice—one suggestion made for each chapter to deepen prayer life.
- Four Scripture verses—ideally, the reader will have or will develop a daily habit of prayer and reflection. These verses—one per week—were selected to inspire ongoing prayer along that month's theme, with plenty of space for journaling from week to week.

Journaling is an important practice, whether reading the book alone or in the context of a small group. Journaling stills the mind, empties it of busy thoughts, and promotes deeper contemplation of the Scripture being read. The free-flowing nature of journaling encourages the mind to surrender to the Holy Spirit and can allow God to speak to us more clearly as we write. Over time, we produce a private record of our thoughts and God's actions in our lives which, when re-read, can deepen our trust in God, Who we see has been working tangibly in our life. The action of journaling is like praying twice, just as singing is thought by some to be "praying twice."

Praying College Moms small groups read a chapter at each monthly meeting and spend time discussing the questions that follow each chapter. Prayer intentions are shared at the beginning or end of each meeting, at the discretion of the team leader. The prayer practice and Scripture Verses are read in between meetings. For more information, see Appendix 2, How to Use This Book in PCM Small Groups.

If reading the book outside of a small group, it is recommended that each chapter be read slowly, pausing for several days after each one to reflect on the questions, journal, and attempt the prayer practice.

All quoted Scripture is from the New American Bible, Revised Edition (NABRE) unless otherwise noted. Stories shared with the author are true, but names have been changed.

The pronoun *him/her* has been chosen arbitrarily for individual chapters, unless otherwise indicated.

PRAYING COLLEGE MOMS PRAYER

DEAR GOD, OUR Father, You have graciously set me over my children as their guardian, their protector, and their first exposure to the faith. With the love of a mother's heart, I have poured myself out teaching, guiding and preparing them for a future of service to You. I am grateful for Your good gifts, especially for the grace You have given me to do my best at parenting.

But now, dear Lord, my child is entering the college-aged years. A new phase of adulthood beckons. Our relationship will change. United with Praying College Moms everywhere, I ask at this time of transition for Your super-abundant blessings on my child and this whole generation of young adults:

- Please make Yourself known to them so that they always believe they are loved, sustained by, and find their purpose in You, dear Lord.
- Help them to master their studies, make good friends, and perhaps discern a career or vocation, according to Your perfect will.

- Keep them safe and temperate in all things.
- Remind them often that their family loves them and prays for them.

With confidence in Your loving Providence, I ask all of these graces through Christ Our Lord, and through the intercession of our Blessed Mother Mary.

To learn more about the organization Praying College Moms see Appendix 1.

FOREWORD

IN 1988, A teenager dressed in all black with heavy black eye makeup refused to receive the Sacrament of Confirmation. Her mother, an Irish Catholic of deep faith and practice, was distraught. Soon after, the teenaged daughter ran away from home and had no contact with the family. The mother prayed. After more than a month, the daughter returned home but shortly after went off to college, an extremely liberal and secular college. The mother prayed more. After being "confirmed" in her pagan unbelief by secular teachers and decadent dorm mates, the daughter went into the world and many years passed. The mother made holy hours in front of the Blessed Sacrament, said her rosary, and invoked the Divine Mercy.

One day, the daughter called her mom and said out of the blue, "Mom, I'm going to be confirmed on Saturday, and I'd like you to be there." "Oh, really," said the Mother with no small bit of trepidation, "In what church will you be confirmed?" The mom pictured Wiccan Priestesses dancing in the moonlight to worship the goddess.

The daughter replied, "In the Catholic Church, of course!" And the mother began to cry tears of joy at the answer to her prayers. The last I heard, the daughter went to Mass daily and was just returning from a weeklong silent retreat in a Trappist monastery.

When you love someone, especially your child, it opens you to suffering. So many dangers, trials, temptations, sins, and sufferings await a young adult in college. ...*And So We Pray 2: Supporting Young Adults Through the College Years* points the way to making the most of these years.

Albert Einstein exaggerated only slightly when he said, "Setting an example is not the main means of influencing another, it is the only means." When we pray regularly, passionately, and earnestly, we make it easier for others to pray and grow closer to God.

When we pray, we make it easier for ourselves to see the good in our children, and not to be overwhelmed by their imperfections. "The way to develop the best that is in a person is by appreciation and encouragement," said Charles Schwab. We can make our own the words of Scripture, "whatever is true, whatever is honorable, whatever is just, whatever is pure, whatever is lovely, whatever is commendable, if there is any excellence, if there is anything worthy of praise, think about these things" in our son or daughter (Phil 4:8). By seeing the good in them, by thanking God for these goods, and by encouraging our children to develop these gifts, we love them and help them.

When we pray, we put our children under the powerful protection of Our Mother in Heaven. When Our Lady of Guadalupe appeared to Juan Diego, she said to him, "Am I not here with you, your mother? Are you not safe in the shadow of my protection? Am I not the source of your life and your happiness? Am I not holding you in my lap, wrapped in my arms? What else can you possibly need? Do not be upset or distressed." Our Lady knew something about distress and sadness, for a sword of sorrow pierced her heart (Luke 2:25). But she also knew the joy of the Resurrection. Her prayer and our prayer is that we all can one day, with all our children, enjoy the unending happiness of heaven. Until then, it's time to pray, helped by this wonderful book.

Dr. Christopher Kaczor is the former William E. Simon Visiting Fellow in Religion and Public Life in the James Madison Program at Princeton University and is Professor of Philosophy at Loyola Marymount University in Los Angeles. Dr. Kaczor's research on issues of ethics, philosophy, and religion has been in the New York Times, the Wall Street Journal, the Los Angeles Times, the Huffington Post, and National Review, as well as on NPR, BBC, EWTN, ABC, NBC, FOX, CBS, MSNBC, TEDx, and The Today Show. He is the author of numerous books, including The Seven Big Myths about the Catholic Church.

I don't remember who threw-up on the door mat, my five-year-old who gagged on her pretzels after watching me throw-up, or me, green with morning sickness, but I do remember being sardonically amused that I had achieved being both nauseated and nauseating in the same afternoon. I remember being much less amused by a neighbor who insisted that I would miss these early parenting years, and further insisted that older children were far more challenging than younger ones. At that point, I had a five-year-old, a three-year-old, a one-year-old and I was expecting another. To complicate matters, the year was 1998 and average women leading average lives lugged their children with them on errands instead of hiring nannies. We shepherded them to grocery stores, pharmacies, dry cleaners and the bank. We ushered them to polling places, Jiffy Lubes and dressing rooms at TJ Maxx where we tried on spring skirts while our three-year-olds helpfully slid under other women's dressing room doors. If you had thirteen kids, you carted thirteen kids to the veterinarian to pick up Mr. Pickles and his eye drops. If you had morning sickness, you carried a sick bag in your minivan and taught the older children to watch the little ones while you dashed into public restrooms to vomit. Sick, tired, emotionally drained, on constant alert for runaway toddlers, I hardly know how I made it through those early years. I was once asked by a public school administrator, after laying down on a bench to wait for my kindergartner, to "please sit in an upright position as laying down sends an unprofessional message to our community." I wanted to respond, "I'm a professional mother, you idiot. Collapsing from exhaustion is part of my job!" Instead, I just sat up—too tired to argue. Enter my neighbor, helpfully informing me that motherhood was going to get worse. I could have spat in her eye. Nineteen years later, however, the truth is that we were both right. With vivid memories of how taxing those early years were, I never tell young mothers that "these are the easy years." But Cynthia was correct, too. Comparatively speaking, they were.

But they also had an advantage that later parenting years don't—books. Books on pregnancy and childbirth. Books about co-sleeping that should have been titled "no-sleeping." Books on the terrible twos. Books about the emerging child. Books on tweens, and books on teens. Books that listed books that might lead you to more helpful books. But no books, that I had yet seen, that acknowledged the challenge of supporting young adults through the college years and suggested ways that a Christian mother might encourage her beloved children into a life-long love affair with Christ by strengthening her own relationship with Him. Until this book. What Maribeth Harper has created in ...*And So We Pray 2* is a space in which mothers can acknowledge their own imperfections and disappointments, their hopes, their fears, and their gratitude while turning resolutely to God for help in shaping their own futures and the futures of their children—*through prayer.*

...*And So We Pray 2* is a book that very much looks forward. It is optimistic, with a confident tone that is the direct result of a firm faith. And it is practical. The Bible, of course, is the ultimate self-help book—meant to be read, studied, and acted upon. ...*And So We Pray 2* brings the Bible into relief with structured reflections, scripture passages, and journaling exercises that facilitate sustained spiritual growth. Additionally, there is a warm community component to Maribeth's book. Faith, of course, is relational, and God is so pleased when Christian women meet to pray and share their faith. This book is such a meeting. The anecdotes Maribeth shares have the power to relieve, comfort, embolden, and, maybe even, subdue us. We mothers are rather famous for our intuitive and our healing powers. Accustomed to being the architects of our children's daily lives, it is tempting to see ourselves as the architects of their spiritual lives as well. Maribeth's book reminds us that as powerful as we are in our children's lives, we cannot will them into a relationship with Christ. Rather, we must present *ourselves* to Christ, in total humility, before we can properly present our children to Him. And so we pray. I cannot imagine a more perfect title for a book about mothering. With two daughters in college next year, this book will be my constant companion. Because Cynthia was right. Older children are harder. After all, the Prodigal Son didn't demand, and then squander, his inheritance when he was three. At three he was sliding under other women's dressing room doors and his mother was thinking: I can't wait until he grows up.

Jennifer Kaczor is the mother of seven children and has written for National Review, Catholic Exchange, Inside Catholic, and the Bellingham Review. She is a contributing author to Chris Kaczor's The Seven Big Myths about Marriage.

CHAPTER 1

ENOUGH ALREADY

JANET PLANNED FOR her family's transition from school days to summer with logistical precision. She wanted hot, nutritious dinners, clean bathrooms (she has four boys), and a long-overdue family vacation. Five drivers competed for two cars, requiring unprecedented familial cooperation. Paying for multiple college tuitions kept she and her husband at work for long hours, making her expectation for the "perfect" summer more than a little challenging. Nevertheless, it started off well. The oldest daughter, newly graduated from college, had begun a job in her field of interest. The family enjoyed a beach vacation, which was relaxing and affordable. "Buster" the dog arrived, promoting teamwork among the siblings, making for lots of laughs and friendly arguments over whose turn it was to walk the dog. Janet managed her youngest child's time so that he was constructively occupied while the others found summer jobs that kept them coming and going... and cash flush. Yet, with the finish line in sight— the return of everyone to their respective schools at the end of August—things began to unravel.

Buster didn't assimilate, as can sometimes happen with dogs who are fostered. He unpredictably lashed out, alternating between sweet family dog and teeth-baring protector, to everyone's dismay. It became clear he needed rehabilitation away from their home—permanently. Janet, the family's most avid dog-lover, arranged for his departure with a heavy heart. Next, Janet's oldest son left two weeks early for college, and Janet was conflicted about a parting observation he had made. Was he unappreciative of Janet's need to work hard to pay for college? Or was Janet, in fact, too committed to the office? Probably both. Sigh… The college junior asked once again if a couple of his friends could come over one night. "Sure," Janet said. Knowing him, she shouldn't have been surprised when fourteen hungry men gathered, ate pizza, and left the den in disarray…again. He would need "a talkin to." Finally, their youngest was back home from a sleep-away camp and called Janet repeatedly at work to remind her he was now bored and "home alone." The chaos was building beyond tolerable levels.

*Enough already…*Janet wanted to cry. All the hard work coordinating the vacation, job transportation, dog duties, and summer camps—not to mention keeping up with a demanding career still resulted in pandemonium and left Janet at her wit's end with fewer than two weeks to go before school started again. Janet wanted someone to listen…to offer advice…to understand! But who? She called on a best friend.

Available at a moment's notice, a best friend listens patiently and attentively to all kinds of troubles explained five different ways, upside down and backward. A best friend sorts through confusion and understands what is meant, not just what is said. A best friend offers wisdom that is perfectly tailored to the unique situation, knowing well the family history and the personalities involved. Full of compassion, a best friend embraces life's messiness and climbs into the trenches with you—every time.

Do you have a friend who fits this description? I do. In fact, we all do. God, our loving Father, listens closely to our every concern, acts wisely, and loves us unconditionally. True, we can't cry on His shoulder or lay our head in His lap [not in this life, anyway] but His reassuring presence can be felt as tangibly. Our best friends are sometimes as busy as we are, but God is never too busy to listen and console us.

So often, our perception of God is what limits our ability to draw close and learn to trust Him. And misperceptions abound! On the one hand, some imagine God as a magician, all sugar and spice and everything nice, showering His friends with every blessing, especially when they're *good enough*. Others view God as a tyrant, shaking His divine finger at them when something goes wrong. Their God-bully is relentless in His judgment and indifferent to their sorrow. In reality, however, God is our Father Who constantly endeavors to show Himself to us, His beloved children. "Call to me, and I will answer you; I will tell you great things beyond the reach of your knowledge." (Jeremiah 33:3).

Is God's friendship *enough* when you find life overwhelming? That depends on how *you* think of God, doesn't it? Stop reading and take a minute or more to come up with five to ten words you would use to describe God. Write them down.

_____   _____

_____   _____

_____   _____

_____   _____

_____   _____

Is the God you described *strong enough, caring enough, attentive enough, or wise enough* to call in a crisis or to ask for a favor? Do you trust Him to care for your college-aged child? Would you ask God to help you with something as simple as finding a parking space at the mall?

GETTING TO KNOW HIM

God, our Father, has bent over backward to help us learn to love and trust Him. He sent His Son, Jesus Christ, to redeem, reconcile and reunite us to the family. He gave us His Holy Spirit to enlighten and empower us after Jesus returned to heaven. He left us His living Word for us to read in the Bible. For two thousand years, God has raised up saints who have radiated His glory so that we can learn from their examples. And God built the church, with its Sacraments, and the Magisterium, to guide and protect us until we rejoin Him for all eternity.

If you want "CliffNotes" —a reliable way to come to know God, and to build up your faith—read the Bible, reflecting on a line or two every day. The Holy Scriptures have been called "God's love letter" to us. Through Scripture God reveals Himself, so much so that the Catechism of the Catholic Church (CCC) teaches, "... such is the force and power of the Word of God that it can serve the Church as her support and vigor, and the children of the Church as strength for their faith, food for the soul, and a pure and lasting fount of spiritual life." (CCC 131).

What does Scripture say to us about Our Father? Here's a sampling:

God is love: "God sent his only Son into the world so that we might have life through him. In this is love: not that we have loved God, but that he loved us and sent his Son as expiation for our sins" (1 John 4:9-10).

God is our creator: "Yet, Lord, you are our father; we are the clay and you our potter: we are all the work of your hand" (Isaiah 64:7).

God is merciful, forgiving us for every wrongdoing, big or small: "Merciful and gracious is the Lord, slow to anger, abounding in mercy. He will not always accuse, and nurses no lasting anger; He has not dealt with us as our sins merit, nor requited us as our wrongs deserve" (Psalm 103:8-10).

God is our provider: "Therefore you are no longer a slave, but a son; and if a son, then an heir through God" (Galatians 4:7). "Do not be afraid any longer, little flock, for your Father is pleased to give you the kingdom" (Luke 12:32). "What eye has not seen, and ear has not heard, and what has not entered the human heart, what God has prepared for those who love him" (1 Corinthians 2:9).

God is our Father, *our Abba.* God's son Jesus lived and died so as to reveal His Father to us. "We have approximately 25,000 words that Jesus spoke recorded in the Bible. Of those 25,000 words, Jesus taught about the Father in Heaven at least 181 times. This means one out of every 140 words, Jesus was speaking about His Father. His central message and purpose was to restore us to a relationship with our Daddy in Heaven."[1] It is Jesus Christ who assures us that God is *enough*:

And I tell you, ask and you will receive; seek and you will find; knock and the door will be opened

---

1 "Top 10 Bible Verses about the Father," *Monday Morning Review,* March 08, 2010, accessed October 17, 2016, https://mondaymorningreview.wordpress.com/2010/03/08/top-10-bible-verses-about-the-father/.

to you. For everyone who asks, receives; and the one who seeks, finds; and to the one who knocks, the door will be opened. What father among you would hand his son a snake when he asks for a fish? Or hand him a scorpion when he asks for an egg? If you then, who are wicked, know how to give good gifts to your children, how much more will the Father in heaven *give the Holy Spirit* to those who ask him?" (Luke 11:9-13) [emphasis added]

Our Father answers our prayers by giving us His Holy Spirit. How is that *enough* when life gets us down? "With the Holy Spirit comes love, joy, peace, patience, kindness, generosity, faithfulness" (Galatians 5:22). The Spirit's infinite patience kicks in when our homesick daughter calls for the third time in as many hours. We are given immeasurable kindness to deal with a son's disappointment over midterm grades. We surprise ourselves with a prudent response to a child's call from college asking for money...again. And, perhaps even more astoundingly, we react with faithfulness and peace when the unexpected happens—an arrest, an accident, or something worse. In the Spirit's strength, we can find supernatural joy in every trial.

The Holy Spirit visited Janet in the weeks after two of her children left for college. The house was calmer, the laundry and grocery-shopping duties had eased, and she was relishing the relative quiet, right? Actually, that's not what happened. Unanticipated financial pressures had arisen, there were surgeries, issues percolating with one child away at school, and the youngest unexpectedly needed more tutoring. Janet's circumstances had not substantially improved. Miraculously, even in the midst of these new challenges, she was peaceful.

"I have finally realized that things are so far beyond my control," she said, "that I have no choice but to trust God with all of this…and it's a good place to be." She wondered aloud whether God had placed her in difficult positions now and at other times in her life precisely so that she would learn to trust Him. "I'm a slow learner, but I think I'm finally getting it," she joked.

Janet hadn't suddenly found the time others have to pray before the Blessed Sacrament or say the rosary regularly. She hadn't seen visions or heard God's voice audibly. But she felt God heard "enough already" and answered her exasperated plea as a prayer. She was renewed in her determination to focus on God's love for her, trusting that God sees and appreciates her efforts to love Him back. And, as meager as she thinks they are, she now rests in the certain hope that her efforts are *enough*.

Prayer

God, my Father, my *Abba*, I praise You for Your awesome power and might and for your gentle and attentive care of me.

More than my husband, Lord, You are enough.
More than my children, Lord, You are enough.
More than my job, Lord, You are enough.
More than any of my life's circumstances, Lord, You are enough.

Only You fulfill me. Help me to realize Your gifts in my life: the gift of the Holy Spirit who bring me peace, patience, and love; the gift of Your Son who died and rose to take away my sins; the gift of your church with Sacraments that cleanse and strengthen me; and the gift of Holy Scripture through which You reveal Yourself to me. You also give me breath and life, family and friends, talents, and many opportunities to share Your love with others. Praised be Your name!

Heavenly Father, bless my child[ren] _____ as they head into the college years. Watch over him and draw him close to You.

Help me to treasure Your presence in my life and end each day with a heart overflowing with gratitude.

Questions for Reflection:

How does your image of God compare to what Jesus tells us about His Father in the Scripture?

What words or phrases describing God do you find most meaningful in times of prayer, joy or sorrow?

Prayer Intentions:

Answered Prayers:

Prayer Practice:
I will be especially attentive while reading Scripture or listening to the Word at Mass for new insight into the nature of God my Father. I will journal any words or phrases that touch my heart.

Lord, how can I love you more today than I did yesterday?

O Lord, our Lord, how awesome is your name through all the earth! Psalm 8:1

Lord, how can I love you more today than I did yesterday?

O Lord, you are our Father; we are the clay, and you are our potter; we are all the work of your hand. Isaiah 64:8

Lord, how can I love you more today than I did yesterday?

Yet you have made [us] little less than a god, crowned [us] with glory and honor. Psalm 8:6

Lord, how can I love you more today than I did yesterday?

The Lord is trustworthy in all his words, and loving in all his works. Psalm 145:13

CHAPTER 2

BETTER THAN THE MOVIES? REAL LIFE WITH GOD...

NOTHING PREPARED VERONICA for the grief she felt when her only son left for college, so she hid in the dark—literally. She took her Costco Skinny Pop popcorn to the movie theater. "I had a lot of time, more than I expected to have or would have liked. Being at home reminded me that I should be cleaning, something I hate with a passion and had been ignoring," she explained. "I was depressed so I went to see nine movies by myself in three weeks. Often, I was the only one in the theater," Veronica recounted.

Veronica says she chose to distract herself with movies because it was something she and her son always enjoyed together. "I would finish the popcorn, and then splurge on Snow Caps because I felt so sorry for me," she laughed. "I told the Lord I just needed to do this until I could get a grip on my life and work through the transition."

When Veronica finally emerged from the dark, she made a beeline for the light, resolutely deciding that her faith in God, which had cooled when prayer slipped from her highest priority, would see her through this tough time. "I began to recognize this time that I had as a golden opportunity to get my spiritual life in order. I've tried before but didn't stick to it," she explained. Buoyed by renewed fervor, Veronica began trying to attend daily Mass more frequently. She found a spiritual director to help her remain accountable to her new resolve. Veronica stopped procrastinating and tackled the deep cleaning and reorganizing she had promised herself she would do, finding strength in her deepening spiritual life. She also committed to praying at the adoration chapel in her parish twice a week for ten to thirty minutes. Spending time before the Blessed Sacrament helped Veronica more than any other devotion at this time in her life, she said.

What does she do there? "I often go in anxious, and I try to spend time in praise and worship, rather than list all the problems I'm having. That helps reset my mood," she said. "Then I tell the Lord, 'Here I am; let's go through this again...' He must be bored with my repeating myself, but I hand it all over the altar to Him. Usually, when I leave, I feel like I really have left my sadness there. Three days later, it's kind of back so I return to the adoration chapel."

"I'm not accustomed to praying in silence and get fidgety," Veronica shared. "It's difficult, but I also find great peace there. By forcing myself to sit, focus, rest, and listen, it has become really fruitful. I am aware that God is handling everything. He's got it all: my son's college career, my daughter's professional life, and my marriage, so I can walk away and feel better."

Veronica roused herself from binging on Hollywood movies at the theater to a pew in the adoration chapel. How did she manage to exchange anxiety and depression for rest and peace? She was called by the light, Jesus Christ. "I am the light of the world. Whoever follows me will not walk in darkness, but will have the light of life" (John 8:12). Of course, not everyone becomes depressed when their children leave for college, nor do we all find time to spare for movie watching. But no matter what your circumstances, God also calls you out of your "darkness"—anxieties about the kids, pressures at work, difficult relationships, health issues—and into His restorative light and a "peace that surpasses all understanding" (Philippians 4:7).

THE CALL INTO LIGHT AND OUR RESPONSE

When you hugged your freshman for a final goodbye, did he return your affection with a manly bear hug? Or cringe and stiffen in embarrassment at the public spectacle? Or was it something in between? God, our Father, reaches out to us with this kind of intense parental love. He prompts our soul interiorly to pray or to act, and He uses all of our surroundings to do so: the beauty of nature, the kindness of others, and sometimes, mysteriously...even our suffering. According to the Catechism of the Catholic Church, "God, infinitely perfect and blessed in himself, in a plan of sheer goodness freely created man to make him share in his own blessed life. For this reason, at every time and in every place, God draws close to man. He calls man to seek him, to know him, to love him with all his strength..." (CCC 1).

How do you respond to God's spiritual hugs? Our greatest treasure in this age of technology and perpetual busyness is the very gift God seeks from each of us: our undivided time and attention through mental prayer. Mental prayer requires our concerted effort. This quiet solitary prayer is an intimate exchange between two: the humble, needy soul and her God. As Veronica discovered, when we sit quietly at adoration, fight off distraction, and try hard to *pay attention,* God makes Himself known.

PRAYER: AN ACT OF LOVE

Any desire we feel to pray has already been placed in our hearts by God who loves us. He inspires us to want to thank Him, praise Him, and, of course, to regularly ask His blessing on our college kids. We correspond to His grace when we commit to consistent daily prayer. Who has time for that? Or is the real question, "Who can afford to miss out?" Modern Psychology touts the emotional benefits of prayer: stress relief, better overall health, faster post-surgical healing, and a happier disposition.[2] But it's

2 "5 Scientifically Supported Benefits of Prayer," *Psychology Today,* June 23, 2014, accessed October 19, 2016, https://www.psychologytoday.com/blog/more-mortal/201406/5-scientifically-supported-benefits-prayer.

the spiritually restorative properties of daily prayer that bring lasting peace.

Five hundred years ago, God sent us a messenger to encourage us in prayer. Her name is Saint Teresa of Avila, and she was a nun, a reformer, and doctor of the church (a trusted expert) on the topic of prayer. She describes prayer this way:

- Mental prayer in my opinion is nothing else than an intimate sharing between friends; it means taking time frequently to be alone with Him who we know loves us.[3]

- However quietly we speak, He is so near that He will hear us: we need no wings to go in search of God, but have only to find a place where we can be alone and look upon Him present within us...we must talk to Him humbly, as we should our father. [4]

- The important thing is not to think much but to love much. [5]

"10 Ways Praying Actually Benefits Your Health!," Health, Fitness, Beauty & Diet, March 20, 2015, accessed October 19, 2016, http://www. thehealthsite.com/diseases-conditions/10-ways-praying-actually-bene-fits-your-health-p114/.

3 Teresa of Avlia, *The Collected Works of Saint Teresa of Avila*, vol.1, trans. Kieran Kavanaugh, OCD and Otilio Rodriguez, OCD (Washington, DC: Institute of Carmelite Studies, 1976), 96.

4 Teresa de Jesús (Teresa of Avila), *The Way of Perfection* (New York: Doubleday, 1991), 184.

5 Teresa of Avila, *The Interior Castle* (New York: Paulist Press, 1979), 70.

WE'RE ALL BEGINNERS

Resolving to set aside a daily time of prayer can be daunting for the beginner, but even the seasoned pray-er—a woman with twenty to forty years of relationship with God—can feel like a toddler as she finds herself needing to recommit over and over to preserving her sacred prayer time. In the simplest of terms, becoming a regular daily pray-er requires that we *set the date, educate,* and *meditate.*

SET THE DATE

What do you prioritize each day? At the top of the list are life's essentials: sleeping, eating, showering, but, what comes next? Care of the family? Work at an office? Exercise? If the list is much too long for a single a day, then perhaps your list is longer than the one God has written for you. How would you know? —By beginning each day with a dedicated ten to fifteen minutes of prayer.

We know that date nights with husbands, coffee klatches with "the girls," and FaceTime with our college kids build relationship. Friends and spouses share a history that builds mutual trust and loyalty. God invites us to "set the date" so He can build with us a reservoir of memories—a history—so that we will look back at the times He has helped, big and small, and learn to trust Him, especially when life gets tough.

"Oh, I pray all day long," my friend Linda said. "I offer little thoughts to God whenever I think about it," she added. That's great, but does she commit to a regular time of prayer? Nope. We talk to husbands or good friends multiple times a day…"Honey, what time will you be here for dinner? I'm going to the store. Can I get you something? Could you drive Tom to practice today?" Those kinds of conversations happen, but they're not soul building. God wants to superabundantly bless us when we pray with focused attention! Listen to the list of spiritual goodies God gives to the woman [or man] who prays:

> In mental prayer, the soul is purified from its sins, nourished with charity, confirmed in faith, and strengthened in hope; the mind expands, the affections dilate, the heart is purified, truth becomes evident; temptation is conquered, sadness dispelled; the senses are renovated; drooping powers revive; tepidity ceases; the rust of vices disappears. Out of mental prayer issues forth, like living sparks, those desires of heaven which the soul conceives when inflamed with the fire of divine love. Sublime is the excellence of mental prayer, great are its privileges; to mental prayer heaven is opened; to mental prayer heavenly secrets are manifested and the ear of God [is] ever attentive. (Saint Peter of Alcantara, spiritual director to Saint Teresa of Avila[6])

---

6 Saint Peter of Alcantara, *Treatise on Prayer*, part 1, in *Conversations with Christ: An Introduction to Mental Prayer*, Rev. Peter-Thomas Rohrback, OCD (Chicago, IL: Fidels Publishers, 1956), 13.

Still, making this commitment to daily prayer takes great faith, doesn't it? We have to believe that when we sit each morning in our comfy chair, perhaps with a cup of coffee and a Bible or prayer book, that God is really present and that He wants to talk with us. When life is especially harried and overwhelming, stopping for fifteen minutes to pray can feel like too much to ask. We can fall prey to allowing "the urgent" to overtake "the important." The enemy can also convince us that prayer really doesn't matter and won't help. Even Saint Teresa succumbed to that temptation. At one point during her years at the convent, she had become so preoccupied with social life in convent's visitor lounge that, convicted by a false humility, the saint resolved to refrain from mental prayer. This was a big mistake, which she rectified with the help of her spiritual director. "This excuse of bodily weakness," she wrote afterward, "was not a sufficient reason why I should abandon so good a thing, which required no physical strength, but only love and habit."[7]

We need love and habit, says Saint Teresa! We are called to set the date "...with a firm determination not to give up, no matter what trials and dryness one may encounter" (CCC 2710).

---

7   "Saint Theresa of Avila," accessed April 13, 2017, http://www.ewtn. com/library/MARY/AVILA.htm. Taken from Father Vann Joseph, *Lives of Saints with Excerpts from Their* Writing, 1954 ed. (New York: John J. Crawley & Co., Inc., 1954).

Educate

When my first son left for college, I began sending care packages of chocolate chip cookies because I knew that he loved these cookies.[8] Now three of my four children live far away, and I continue to mail care packages occasionally, full of their favorite things. I know what they like because I have spent a lifetime learning their preferences. Similarly, God encourages us to get to know Him; what pleases Him, what He desires for us, and what He has in store for us for all eternity! He has sent us some love letters to read—His Living Word in the Scriptures. By praying in little increments using the Scriptures, especially the Gospels, God reveals Himself to us through Jesus Christ, and He also teaches us plenty about ourselves! We are also blessed with more than two thousand years of church tradition, treatises like the Catechism of the Catholic Church, and the living witness of the saints to help us learn about God.

Does it seem odd that God would "require" us to *educate* ourselves about spiritual things? Why doesn't He just infuse this knowledge into our souls? The simple answer is "love." By setting the date, and educating ourselves about God, we are exercising our free will which is the single greatest gift God gives us. By choosing God over worldly distractions, by carving out precious moments reading

---

8 Praying College Moms Care Packages are delivered every November to hundreds of college students all over the country. For more information or to order, see prayingcollegemoms.org.

His love letters, and by thinking about Him, we prove our love for Him…which brings us to the next point….

MEDITATE

Meditation has become popular, newsworthy, and mainstream. "We all need to get a little head space," says Headspace founder Andy Puddicombe.[9] Headspace is among the top five smart phone apps, with an alleged six million subscribers.[10] Yogis encourage meditation as do tai chi and qi gong instructors. A Harvard Medical School blog post references a study providing evidence that meditation is more beneficial than vacation.[11]

Citing unprecedented anxiety among college students,[12] a web search reports these top five of fifty

---

9   "Man behind meditation app goes from monk to millionaire," *Telegraph*, accessed October 31, 2016, http://www.telegraph.co.uk/men/the-filter/11154773/Man-behind-meditation-app-goes-from-monk-to-millionaire.html.

10   "How Andy Puddicombe, Monk-Turned-Entrepreneur, Brought Meditation to the Masses," *Huffpost*, accessed October 31, 2016, http://www.huffingtonpost.com/entry/andy-puddicombe-headspace-meditation_us_570bbb68e4b0836057a1ac66.

11   Editor-in-Chief, Harvard Health Publications et al.,"Regular Meditation More Beneficial than Vacation," *Harvard Health Blog RSS*, October 27, 2016, accessed November 02, 2016, http://www.health.harvard.edu/blog/relaxation-benefits-meditation-stronger-relaxation-benefits-taking-vacation-2016102710532.

12   The American College Health Association found in a 2015 study that 85.6 percent of respondents felt overwhelmed by their responsibilities. American College Health Association, American College Health Association-National College Health Assessment II: Reference Group

leading campuses have designated space for student meditation.

- The Bartlett Reflection Center at DePauw University
- Skidmore College—Gazebo on Haupt Pond
- The Cornell Plantations in Ithaca, New York
- Colgate University—Chapel House
- The Danforth Chapel at the University of Kansas[13]

While contemporary culture may acknowledge that meditation is good for us, an important distinction must be made between present-day "meditation" and the sacred appointment Our Lord makes with us each morning in those moments of quiet reflection from our prayer chair. All Christian meditation is oriented toward God, as revealed to us through the Scriptures. Christians give their time and attention as a gift to God who loves them both personally and universally. Christians work to empty their mind not for its own sake, but to make room for the Holy Spirit. In Christian meditation, no mantra is chanted, nor does the pray-er necessarily sit or stand a

Executive Summary Spring 2015 (Hanover, MD: American College Health Association, 2015).

13 "The 50 Best Campus Meditation Spaces.," Best Counseling Schools, October 2015, accessed November 01, 2016, http://www.bestcounseling-schools.org/best-campus-meditation-spaces.

certain way. Christians seek interior silence to hear the voice of God who whispers.[14]

No mantra, no yoga poses, no breathing techniques? How do Christians meditate? Fifteen minutes can feel like an eternity for a soul learning or struggling for any number of reasons to pray. Because we are only human, applying a little structure to the time set aside for prayer can help. One of the best guides for spending prayer time well suggests that we Concentrate, Consider, Converse, and Commit.[15]

Using a short passage from the Gospel,

- Concentrate: Quiet your mind, relax, and speak to God. Ask for grace to hear Him
- Consider: Read and reread the lines from the Gospel you chose, asking for inspiration
- Converse: When a line of the Gospel moves you, praise God, adore Him, express your sorrow for sin, thank Him, and/or ask for what you and your family need
- Commit: Renew your commitment to God, to prayer, and to whatever inspirations and resolutions He has given you in your time of prayer

---

14 1 Kings 19: 11-13.

15 Father John Bartunek, LC, *The Better Part* (Hamden, CT: Circle Press, 2007). Front and back cover flap.

God shows up whenever we pray, no matter how we pray, as long as we make the effort! As Veronica learned during her time at adoration, even if our senses don't perceive Him, the "peace that surpasses all understanding" (Philippians 4:7) is a sure sign God has visited us. In fact, the Holy Spirit brings fruits every time we meditate: love, joy, peace, patience, kindness, generosity, faithfulness, gentleness, self-control (Galatians 5:22-23). Which one of us can afford to miss out?

Prayer

Dear Heavenly Father, You created the universe—the moon, the stars, and the sun—and all the creatures of the Earth. I am humbled, awed and grateful that you invite me to meet You whenever I pray.

I want to commit myself to praying regularly, with great fervor, because I know it pleases You, and prayer changes me, transforming me more closely to Your image and likeness. Please give me this grace.

Help me, with a better understanding of your personal love for me, to weather the transition of sending my child _____ into the next phase of his/her life. With your grace, I will be a cheerful, peaceful, witness to my child and his/her friends, as well as to everyone you place in my path from this day forward.

Questions for Reflection:

What kinds of emotional factors keep me from praying regularly (or if I'm praying daily, more intentionally)? Tiredness? Melancholy? Lack of faith? What steps can I take to strengthen this commitment to God?

God works through our memories and experiences. I will share with the group and/or journal about times God has answered my prayers, surprised me with an unexpected gift, or lifted my spirits in suffering.

What is my favorite way to pray/meditate? I will share with the group and/or journal about what works well for me and what kinds of obstacles I experience.

Prayer Intentions:

Answered Prayers:

Prayer Practice:
I will strive to keep my daily appointment with God every day this week...and then every day next week, etc.

Lord, how can I love you more today than I did yesterday?

...let hearts that seek the LORD rejoice! Psalm 105:3

Lord, how can I love you more today than I did yesterday?

Seek out the LORD and his might; constantly seek his face. Psalm 105:4

_____

_____

_____

_____

_____

_____

_____

_____

_____

_____

_____

_____

_____

_____

_____

_____

_____

_____

_____

Lord, how can I love you more today than I did yesterday?

Recall the wondrous deeds he has done, his wonders and words of judgment... Psalm 105:5

Lord, how can I love you more today than I did yesterday?

I praise your name for your mercy and faithfulness. For you have exalted over all your name and your promise. Psalm 138:2

CHAPTER 3

"HOW IS CLASS? ARE YOU GOING TO MASS?"

DRIVING HOME WITH my soon-to-be-freshman son from a precollege orientation program late one evening, he said something I will never forget. Perhaps encouraged by the excitement of the orientation, the anticipation of heading off to college, or the intimacy of the warm, cozy car shielding us from the frigid night, he took the opportunity to thank me. "I am ready to go to college," he told me confidently. "And I am so grateful to you and Dad." He shared with me how grounded he felt by the support of our family, how appreciative he was for the gift of education, and, most importantly, how grateful he was to have received the faith, which enabled him to trust God with his future. That is a memory I truly cherish.

Ten years later, he still feels the loving support of his family, and, having nearly completed a master's program, he continues to appreciate the value of education. Sadly, however, he no longer practices his Catholic faith. Although the Sacraments were readily available during his four years at a Catholic college, he stopped going to Mass and then left the church altogether before he graduated. I became one of so many mothers wondering how their children, who were raised Catholic and went to Mass every Sunday, abandoned the faith during college.

Dwindling Mass attendance is not unique to millennials on college campuses. In today's society, people of all faiths are gradually shifting away from formalized religion to self-professed "nones," according to a Gallup Organization 2016 study.[16] In fact, Gallup's "longest-running religious service attendance question asks, 'Did you, yourself, happen to attend church, synagogue or mosque in the last seven days, or not?' In 1939, when Gallup first asked this question, 41% said 'yes.' That percentage dropped to 37% in 1940 and rose to 39% in 1950. It continued to climb, reaching as high as 49% at multiple points in the 1950s. Attendance then settled down to figures around 40% for decades, before dropping to 36% for the past three years."[17]

"Everyone is doing it" doesn't assuage a mother's feelings of helplessness as she watches an adult child drift away from the foundational beliefs she worked so hard to teach him as a youth. We know parents are the first educators of their children in the faith, and Saint Pope John Paull II tells us we are well equipped for the job. "For Christian parents the mission to educate, a mission

---

16 Frank Newport, "Five Key Findings on Religion in the U.S.," Gallup. com, December 23, 2016, accessed January 10, 2017, http://www.gallup. com/poll/200186/five-key-findings-religion.aspx.
17 Ibid.

rooted, as we have said, in their participation in God's creating activity, has a new specific source in the sacrament of marriage, which consecrates them for the strictly Christian education of their children: that is to say, it calls upon them to share in the very authority and love of God the Father and Christ the Shepherd, and in the motherly love of the Church, and it enriches them with wisdom, counsel, fortitude and all the other gifts of the Holy Spirit in order to help the children in their growth as human beings and as Christians."[18]

We have our children baptized, they receive First Holy Communion and Confirmation, we make financial sacrifices to send them to good schools, take them to Mass faithfully, and teach them the faith to the best of our ability...and still they stray. "Did I send him to the wrong college? Was it my parenting? Is secular society just too powerful of an influence?" a concerned mother might wonder.

When children are little, Vacation Bible School, CCD, and Veggie Tales can reinforce the faith lessons we strive to teach them. As they grow into young adults, so does their discernment. Belief in God is no longer taught as much as it is "caught." At this age, nagging and hand wringing can dangerously erode our most persuasive

18 Pope John Paul, II, Familiaris Consortio (November 22, 1981) #38, accessed January 10, 2017, http://w2.vatican.va/content/john-paul-ii/en/apost_exhortations/documents/hf_jp-ii_exh_19811122_familiaris-consortio.html.

means of getting teens to Mass: our joyful witness. Buoyed by fidelity to prayer and little hidden sacrifices, our joyful witness is what draws the firepower of the Holy Spirit into the souls of our fallen-away children. And so we ask ourselves: Is our own fervor for the Mass so contagious that those around us can't help but become "infected" with the love of the Eucharist? Do they see us genuflecting reverently, singing along, listening to the Word proclaimed, and praying with head bowed after Communion? Do we share in natural and loving ways what impact the Mass has on our lives? Do our lives reflect a confidence and dependence on the Lord in the Eucharist? Are we as convinced as the saints are about the spiritual gifts that await us at every celebration of the Mass?

Julie, a young mother from my parish, recently gave a compelling personal testimony about the Mass to her Bible-study group. "Nine months ago," she said, "I prayed a specific prayer asking for the desire to begin going to daily Mass." Shortly thereafter, Julie took the heroic step of bringing her rambunctious two-year-old to Mass. "It was a miserable experience at first" she conceded. "My son was noisy and distracting, and I left feeling defeated more often than not." Within weeks, however, her zeal began to grow. "Do you realize that every Mass brings us divine healing, renewed strength, and transformation?" she asked. "I wish I had known that when my kids were even younger. I could have used those graces!" she laughed. She then shared a concrete example from her life of healing, strengthening, and transformation she said she has received from the Eucharist at Mass.

What young college student wouldn't benefit from a healing of social anxieties so prevalent on campus, or a strengthening to study longer and harder, or a transformation into a more peaceful, balanced, and happy student? Those graces are free for the taking at every Mass. "Healing, strength, and transformation" are the answers to a teen's question, "I don't get anything out of Mass so why should I go?"

Why do you go to Mass? If you're not sure of the answer, or if, like most of us, you find yourself occasionally writing grocery lists, reviewing the day's calendar, or otherwise mentally absent in our pew, reflect on what these great church leaders and saints have to say about the Mass...Then, like Julie did, humbly ask for the grace of zeal for Our Lord in the Eucharist through the celebration of the Holy Mass.

- The Mass is the most perfect form of prayer. (Pope Pius VI)
- The celebration of the Mass is as valuable as Jesus's death on the cross. (Saint Thomas Aquinas, Doctor of the Church)
- The heavens open and multitudes of angels come to assist in the Holy Sacrifice of the Mass. (Saint Gregory, Doctor of the Church)
- If we really understood the Mass we would die of joy. (Saint John Vianney)

- Put all the good works in the world against a Holy Mass; they would be as a grain of sand beside a mountain. (Saint John Vianney)
- It would be easier for the world to survive without the sun than to do without Holy Mass. (Saint Padre Pio)
- When Mass is celebrated the sanctuary is filled with countless angels who adore the divine victim immolated on the altar. (Saint John Chrysostom)
- Without doubt, the Lord grants all favors asked of Him in Mass, provided they be fitting for us. (Saint Jerome, Doctor of the Church)
- There is nothing so great as the Eucharist. If God had something more precious, He would have given it to us. (Saint John Vianney)
- What graces, gifts and virtues the Holy Mass calls down. (Saint Leonard of Port Maurice[19])
- It is not to remain in a golden ciborium that He comes down each day from Heaven, but to find another Heaven, the Heaven of our soul in which He takes delight. (Saint Thérèse of Lisieux, Doctor of the Church)

---

19   RomanCatholic33, "The Catholic Mass," July 13, 2010, accessed January 10, 2017, https://www.youtube.com/watch?v=CJtRXzyWul8&feature=youtu.be.

- If angels could be jealous of men, they would be so for one reason: Holy Communion. (Saint Maximilian Kolbe[20])
- Christ is always present in His Church, especially in her liturgical celebrations. He is present in the Sacrifice of the Mass not only in the person of his minister...but especially in the Eucharistic species...He is present in His word since it is He Himself who speaks when the holy Scriptures are read in the Church...He is present when the Church prays and sings, for He has promised "where two or three are gathered together in my name there am I in the midst of them." (Matthew 18:20; CCC 1088)

---

20   "Quotes on the Most Blessed Sacrament," Real Presence Eucharist Education and Adoration Association, accessed January 10, 2017, http://www.therealpresence.org/eucharst/tes/a7.html.

Prayer

Heavenly Father, in the words of the second Eucharist Prayer read at Mass, "It is truly right and just, our duty and our salvation, always and everywhere to give you thanks... and so, with the Angels and all the Saints [I] declare your glory..."

Lift the veil that covers my human eyes and reveal to me the limitless supernatural beauty of the Holy Mass. Empowered by Your grace, enable me to receive Your body and blood in Holy Communion with ever-increasing reverence so that I am healed, strengthened and transformed, according to Your will.

By my transformation, allow my peace and joy to overflow upon my loved ones, especially _____. When I am provoked by worry and tempted to nag or pester _____ by asking, "Are you going to Mass tonight?" or "How was the homily," or any variation of "Remember, Sunday Mass is not optional..." please "set a guard, Lord, before my mouth, keep watch over the door of my lips" (Psalm 141:3).

Help me, Lord, to depend on You by praying faithfully, offering sacrifices, and living my own very unique version of joyful Christianity, so that _____ cannot help but be attracted to You. I live for Your glory, Lord.

Questions for Reflection:

Which of the quotes about the Mass from saints and/or doctors of the church most inspire me? Why?

The church teaches that we have a serious obligation to attend Mass every Sunday and on Holy Days of Obligation (CCC 2180). Do I attend Mass every Sunday, even on vacations or when there are conflicts with sports or other familial activities?

Prayer Intentions:

Answered Prayers:

Prayer Practice:
I will read and reflect on the Eucharistic Prayer II, which is the most common Eucharistic Prayer used during Mass, and is oriented to God our Father. (This prayer can be found in a missal used during the Mass, or in the *Magnificat.*)

Lord, how can I love you more today than I did yesterday?

While they were eating, he took bread, said the blessing, broke it, and gave it to them, and said, "Take it; this is my body." Then he took a cup, gave thanks, and gave it to them, and they all drank from it. He said to them, "This is my blood of the covenant, which will be shed for many. Mark 14:22-24

Lord, how can I love you more today than I did yesterday?

The grace of the Lord Jesus Christ and the love of God and the fellowship of the holy Spirit be with all of you. 2 Corinthians 13

Lord, how can I love you more today than I did yesterday?

Pray then like this:
Our Father who art in heaven,
Hallowed be thy name.
Thy kingdom come.
Thy will be done,
On earth as it is in heaven.
Give us this day our daily bread;
And forgive us our debts,
As we also have forgiven our debtors;
And lead us not into temptation,
But deliver us from evil. Matthew 6:9-13

Lord, how can I love you more today than I did yesterday?

And Jesus went with them, but when he was only a short distance from the house, the centurion sent friends to tell him, "Lord, do not trouble yourself, for I am not worthy to have you enter under my roof. Therefore, I did not consider myself worthy to come to you; but say the word and let my servant be healed. Luke 7:6-7

CHAPTER 4

STRESSING OUT...IT'S SO...MILLENNIAL

DOCTOR SMITH SEES hundreds of students at the large state university where she works, "and many of them are very stressed out," she says. Other than the garden-variety cold, flu, or UTI, she sees at the clinic, students come in with non-specific abdominal pains, insomnia, palpitations, and other inexplicable symptoms that boil down to one diagnosis: stress.

"These days I think there is a lot more pressure on students. I don't know whether it's 'getting the right job' pressure or 'succeeding in school' pressure or pressures from comparing themselves to others on social media, but it's ironic...they achieve academically, they try to eat healthfully, and then they go out on the weekends, drink too much, and engage in high-risk behavior that stresses them out," she says. The treatment can vary but usually starts with a conversation opener like, "Tell me what's going on with you," the doctor says. If the student choses to open up and share, the doctor offers reassurance and counsel. She can also refer the student, as necessary, to the university's counseling center or the mental health clinic.

The doctor's observations are confirmed by studies concluding that millennials are a very stressed-out generation! Stress and/or anxiety are the most highly reported causes of a decline in academic performance among college students, according to the American College Health Association. At some point during a twelve-month period in 2015, nearly 86 percent of students reported feeling overwhelmed, 82 percent felt exhausted (not from physical exercise), 58 percent felt lonely, and 48 percent felt hopeless.[21] For the sixth year in a row, college mental health clinicians across the country are seeing an uptick in the number of students being treated for stress-related issues.[22]

When college students call home complaining of sleepless nights or non-specific aches and pains, parents can find it difficult to know whether medical intervention is required or a little TLC will fix the problem. Four quick assessments can help to determine how stressed she really is.

1. Is she eating well? Many millennials have become rigid about what foods they eat. They consume an average of 20 percent less snack food than their

---

21 "Reference Group Executive Summary Spring 2015," accessed January 26, 2017, http://www.acha-ncha.org/docs/NCHA- II_WEB_ SPRING_2015_REFERENCE_GROUP_EXECUTIVE_SUMMARY.pdf.

22 *2016 Annual Report*, report, (State College, PA: Center for Collegiate Mental Health, Penn State University), 9, accessed January 26, 2017, https://sites.psu.edu/ccmh/files/2017/01/2016-Annual-Report-FINAL_2016_01_09-1gc2hj6.pdf.

parents.[23] Fueled by opinion sharing and picture taking via social media, today's youth "have developed values for or against certain food groups."[24] Food is either good or bad. Sugar is "out." Fresh ingredients are "in." They prefer exotic produce when it's available.[25] Have your college students developed a hankering for papaya, dragonfruit, passionfruit, ataulfo mangoes, young coconuts, or Kiwano melons? At the state university where she works, Doctor Smith said many students avail themselves of produce from a weekly farmer's market that comes to the campus. She also said, however, that students tend to make wise food choices during the week and binge on pizza and beer over the weekend.

2. Is she sleeping long enough? A good night sleep (seven to nine hours) promotes learning, memory retention, emotional balance, problem solving and creativity. Jawbone, the maker of a sleep tracker, monitored 1.4 million nights of sleep on college campuses and found that students get slightly more than seven hours of sleep per

23 "Millennials and Food," (College of Tropical Agriculture and Human Resources, University of Hawaii at M noa), 2, accessed on January 26, 2017, http://www.ctahr.hawaii.edu/oc/freepubs/pdf/FST-63.pdf.

24 Ibid.

25 ibid.

night on average.[26] That's good news, right? Their "night" of sleep usually begins after midnight, however. Don't be surprised to find that your college student goes to bed at college between 12:30 a.m. and 1:30 a.m. on weeknight, but much later on weekends, making it more difficult to get back on track for the next school week.

If she complains she's chronically tired, you might ask about stimulant use or abuse. Adderall, caffeine, and energy drinks are commonly misused on campus to prepare for finals, or to get up for class after a late night of partying. Overuse leads to chronic fatigue. Familiarize yourself with the college website so that you can recommend one or more of the abundant on-campus resources available at most colleges to properly diagnose her fatigue.

3. Is she exercising regularly? Students who exercise score higher GPAs, according to studies by Purdue University and Michigan State University.[27] "[The

26 Brian Wilt, "How University Students Sleep," *The Jawbone Blog*, March 20, 2016, accessed on January 30, 2017, https://jawbone.com/blog/university-students-sleep

27 "College students working out at campus gyms get better grades," Purdue University, April 15, 2013, accessed on January 30, 2017, https://www.purdue.edu/newsroom/releases/2013/Q2/college-students-working-out-at-campus-gyms-get-better-grades.html.
"Want a higher GPA in College? Join a Gym," Michigan State University, July 10, 2014, accessed on January 30, 2017, http://msutoday.msu.edu/news/2014/want-a-higher-gpa-in-college-join-a-gym.

gym] is a place where students learn to use physical activity to cope with stress," says Tricia Zelaya, assistant director for student development and assessment at Purdue's Division of Recreational Sports.[28] Purdue has a newly renovated 355,000 square feet facility with a twelve-hundred-square-foot cycling center, a recreational pool, climbing and bouldering walls, designated racquetball and wallyball courts, an indoor hockey and soccer court, and running tracks.[29] Not every school is so well equipped, but colleges have spent more than $1.7 billion since 2010 expanding or updating their recreational facilities.[30] What excuse can there be for *not* exercising, especially since most facilities are just steps from the undergraduate dorms?

4. Is she managing her time appropriately? Doctor Christina Lynch claims that millennials are "overconnected." Sending more than one thousand texts a day, they rely too heavily on social media, which isolates them with thousands of "friends."[31]

---

28 "College students working out at campus gyms get better grades," Purdue University, April 15, 2013, accessed on January 30, 2017, https://www.purdue.edu/newsroom/releases/2013/Q2/college-students-working-out-at-campus-gyms-get-better-grades.html.

29 Ibid.

30 Ibid.

31 Christina Lynch, *Millennials, Professional Resource Guide,* (Arlington, VA: Divine Mercy University, 2016), 11.

As a result, their attention span is short, they get easily bored, and they can lack the self-discipline required for a work/life balance, says the psychologist. The way to motivate millennials, she says, is to appeal to their desire for purpose and meaning in what they do. Millennials rise to challenges and long to be inspired. They function better when they see their daily tasks in light of something bigger. As their parents, we can help them by providing a supernatural and practical everyday context for the hard work they do.

A SPIRITUAL ANTIDOTE TO STRESS

At her university clinic, Doctor Smith sees stressed-out students in her office as often as they feel they need to come in. "We try to arrange it so the students consult with the same doctor time after time so we get to know their story," she explained. One recent case, however, needed no referral, no prescription, no professional counseling to resolve itself. The young lady experienced a complete relief from stress—a drug-free, intervention-less 100 percent recovery in twenty-four hours.

The freshman was an international student, her family's only child, from an elite group of the best and brightest sent to this country to study, the doctor explained. "She had been coming in to see me, presenting with gastrointestinal symptoms resulting from anxiety and from restricting her food intake too much," said the doctor, "and we had been trying to work through these issues together." One day, after several visits, the freshman came to the clinic to ask Doctor Smith a surprising question. "Do you believe in Jesus Christ?" she asked. The student told her doctor that she had met Jesus Christ through a friend who had taken her to church. "Now" she said, "I know that it doesn't matter what my parents think, or what my teachers think, or what anyone else thinks. Jesus loves me for who I am," she exclaimed joyfully. That was her last visit to the health center, Doctor Smith said.

Admittedly, instantaneous conversions like these are rarely reported, but the fact remains that the Great Physician can unburden our children (and us) just as miraculously. When we are faithful to prayer, Christ heals and restores us—sometimes dramatically, sometimes imperceptibly over a longer period of time. The Lord blesses our efforts to draw close, filling us with the freedom and joy this student felt. We can't help but pass it along to our own college students. Joy is contagious!

Saint Paul was mission driven like many of our modern-day millennials. For his "cause," the Gospel of Jesus Christ, Saint Paul was beaten, shipwrecked, robbed and in "danger from bandits, danger from my own people, danger from Gentiles, danger in the city, danger in the wilderness, danger at sea, danger from false brothers and sisters; in toil and hardship, through many a sleepless night, hungry and thirsty, often without food, cold and naked" (2 Corinthians 11:24-27). He persevered because "Christ Jesus has made me his own" (Philippians 3:12). Saint Paul knew he was loved by Jesus. Are you as confident in the love Jesus has for you?

How often do you reflect on the fact that you are "fearfully and wonderfully made?" (Psalm 139:14)...That you are made in God's image (Genesis 1:27)...That you are "little less than a god," and "crowned with glory and honor" (Psalm 8:6)...That you were adopted by the King of Kings when you were baptized? (CCC 1265). Do these facts bring you joy? "True happiness is not found in riches or well-being, in human fame or power, or in any human achievement— however beneficial it may be—such as science, technology, and art, or indeed in any creature, but in God alone, the source of every good and of all love..." (CCC 1723).

This joy we receive from the Holy Spirit through prayer (Galatians 5:22) is transmitted to our college students when they sense that our confidence is anchored in Christ and can't easily be shaken. Our advice is inspired and wise,[32] grounded in what's best for them, not influenced by fear or anxiety. Our interactions with our child are marked by playfulness, laughter, and a spirit of fun. They sense the joy we have in their company because we're not tied up in knots wondering if they're going to Mass or

---

32 "If any of you is lacking in wisdom, ask God, who gives to all generously and ungrudgingly, and it will be given you" (James 1:5).

getting good grades. We've removed ourselves from the "driver's seat" of their lives, allowing the Lord, who loves them more than we ever will, to take the steering wheel. And from our new perspective—on our knees, close to Christ—we find life is a lot more en*joy*able. He is in control!

What is this joy? Is it having fun? ... Having fun is good. But joy is more, it is something else. It is something that does not come from short term economic reasons, from momentary reasons: it is something deeper. It is a gift...Joy is a gift from God. It fills us from within. It is like an anointing of the Spirit. And this joy is the certainty that Jesus is with us and with the Father.[33]

---

33 Pope Francis, "Christian Joy Far from Simple Fun," transcript, Vatican Radio, October 5, 2013.

Prayer

Dear God, Father, Son and Holy Spirit, You are Love incarnate, Giver of all good gifts. Bless my child _____ and protect _____ from being too stressed at college. Help me to discern how to best help _____ if he/she asks.

Bless me with a contagious joy—the fruit of your Spirit within me. I need this supernatural virtue; a joy that overflows to those around me, especially my child _____. By your grace, I want to be wise and loving, living each day with a playful, authentic spirit of joy. I ask for a joy that empowers me to serve my family and accomplish my duties cheerfully.

Finally, Lord, help me to be faithful to my time of prayer, recognizing that the joy I ask for comes from listening to, knowing, loving and serving You as a beloved daughter of the most High King!

Questions for Reflection:

How does the virtue of joy counteract the tendency to become overwhelmed or stressed-out? Read Appendix 3: Ten Weeks to Finding Joy and discuss or journal.

Eutrapelia is a virtue related to joy that directs us to relax and have fun in such a way that our minds, bodies and souls are truly refreshed. How do I relax? Do I know what kinds of activities refresh me? Our Lord gave us Sundays as a day of rest. He gives us "permission" to practice eutraphelia at the very least on that one day a week! Discuss (or journal about) some ways to make Sundays a time of rest for the whole family.

Prayer Intentions:

Answered Prayers:

Prayer Practice:
Although he endured many hardships for the Gospel, Saint Paul did not complain. In imitation of him, I will strive to replace every complaint with (1) silence, (2) a positive comment, or (3) a prayer of praise as recommended in 1 Thessalonians 5:18.

Lord, how can I love you more today than I did yesterday?

Rejoice always, pray without ceasing, give thanks in all circumstances; for this is the will of God in Christ Jesus for you. 1 Thessalonians 5:16-18

Lord, how can I love you more today than I did yesterday?

But you are merciful to all, for you can do all things, and you overlook people's sins, so that they may repent. Wisdom 11: 23

Lord, how can I love you more today than I did yesterday?

For you love all things that exist, and detest none of the things that you have made, for you would not have made anything if you had hated it. How would anything have endured if you had not willed it? Or how would anything not called forth by you have been preserved? You spare all things, for they are yours, O Lord, you who love the living. Wisdom 11: 24-26

Lord, how can I love you more today than I did yesterday?

The Father is the source of joy. The Son is its manifestation, and the Holy Spirit its giver. – Message of Pope Francis for World Mission Day 2014

CHAPTER 5

A WILL AND A WAY

THE DAY THAT Brian's father unexpectedly died, his mother returned to prescription drug use and alcohol. The fourteen-year-old was headed for foster care on the small tropical island he called home, which seemed like anything but paradise to Brian. The Lord, however, had a marvelously different plan.

Two thousand miles away, Brian's aunt Marypat and her husband John were in the throes of college decision making for their daughter, a senior in high school. Their older son was a junior in college at the time. Hefty college bills kept John and Marypat at work for long hours but they were proud of their children's accomplishments and felt blessed to have been able to provide them with a quality education—something the couple set as a high priority for the family.

Hearing of her brother's unexpected death, Marypat was devastated and felt compelled to intervene. With John's wholehearted support, she decided to try to bring Brian home to their Washington, DC, suburb, acknowledging that it would be a tough transition for him. They hadn't spent time with Brian since he was two years old. Marypat and John would face major familial shift, make a radical commitment to parenting a virtual stranger, and take on an unanticipated financial burden, including another four years of college tuition one day. To hear Marypat tell it, three of them arrived that day in 2008 to meet Brian, plead his case in court, and bring him home: Marypat, John, and Saint Thérèse of Lisieux.

"Thérèse of Lisieux was the saint I chose for Confirmation," Marypat explained, "and I have always prayed to her. My good friend, Judy, knew this, and during those difficult days preparing to meet Brian and hopefully bring him home with us, Judy encouraged me to ask Thérèse for a rose as a sign that things would work out according to God's plan. I had never asked for a sign, nor did I know that Thérèse of Lisieux was famous for showering her spiritual friends with roses! But on the plane to meet Brian, I prayed for the sign, because Judy told me to, and for peace and reassurance that we were doing the right thing."

Marypat said her heart was pounding as she heard Brian's footsteps bound up the stairs to the office in which they were to meet. He rounded the corner carrying a single artificial red rose, which he presented to her as a greeting. When she asked, Brian explained that he had found the rose on the floor in the jewelry store below the office and thought to bring it as a gift. Marypat further investigated and found no explainable source for the rose—Her beloved Thérèse had been accompanying her. "The peace was surreal and I felt a renewed confidence that Brian would be moving in with us," Marypat said.

With legal custody sealed, the family welcomed Brian in January 2009, to his new home in a neighborhood steps from the local Catholic grade school and church. However, troubles continued. Marypat was hoping Brian would repeat eighth grade, but the principal refused to accept him at all because of his prior poor academic performance. "Since I live across the street from the school, it was clearly the best option to help Brian integrate into the community, so I was devastated at the news," Marypat said. Next, Brian's grandmother, (Marypat's mom) became seriously ill with cancer. Brian's mom, they realized, was also dying. "It was more than any human being could have dealt with, but I just kept praying," said Marypat. She also kept advocating. Marypat visited the pastor who overturned the principals' decision and opened the doors to Brian as the winter break ended. Whew!

No sooner had they started to feel their land legs than preparations for high school had to be made. Grades could not be leveraged, but Brian excelled at baseball, just as his father had in college. Those hopes were dashed as Brian was rejected from the high school his stepbrother had attended. Undaunted, Marypat armed herself with eight pages of handwritten notes and the power of Thérèse of Lisieux. She requested a meeting with the headmaster. "I was sure it was the place for him and felt pushed by some supernatural force to get him in there," she said. Brian was admitted in June.

The troubles did not cease. Brian's mother died in 2010 of liver cancer. Marypat's mother's health grew worse. "There were so many funerals, and so much sadness, I really don't know how Brian managed," Marypat said. Evidently, God was using these circumstances to bring Brian, who had been completely uncatechized, to the Catholic faith. At age sixteen, he added RCIA[34] to his already challenging academic load. "He was like a sponge," said Marypat. "I think the faith really helped him process all of his losses in a healthy way," she added. One year later, on Good Friday, 2012, Marypat's mother died. The next day, Brian was baptized and received his First Holy Communion and Confirmation. Buoyed by those graces, Brian and his family in June faced the sudden death of Brian's uncle, age fifty-six (Marypat's brother who died of a massive heart attack while taking a shower). "I think we all grew in faith even though it was a really painful period," said Marypat.

Marypat called Saint Thérèse back into action that fall when it came time to look for a college for Brian. Marypat and John had vowed Brian would receive every advantage their two children had, which included debt-free college education. Marypat was insistent that the education be top-notch, and Brian wanted to play baseball but knew

---

34 Rite of Catholic Initiation for Adults

little else about the American college application process. Many of the schools interested in Brian were too
expensive. Marypat prayed. In late March, on their way
to a baseball game, their coach invited them to look at a
nearby school. The school's president was originally from
the D.C. area and knew Brian's coach. They looked at the
school as one among several options, but they had a "good
feeling" about it.

Marypat pursued financial aid and set up a few meetings one spring day with the school. She knew it wasn't
going to work if they couldn't obtain some financial assistance. Praying while driving there, Marypat stopped at a
hotel to check in and prepare for her meetings. She was
greeted at the door of her room with a fresh red rose,
hanging from the knob with a sign welcoming her as a
new customer. Apparently, that's how they welcomed every
new guest, but Marypat's was the only door that morning
so adorned. Marypat knew Saint Thérèse was interceding
again. Two weeks later, the day she finished a novena, a
letter from the school arrived with the scholarship offer
they needed to make things work.

Brian is now a senior in college, a regular at Sunday
Mass on campus, playing baseball, and looking forward
to a career in lobbying or government. Marypat and John
are ready to take a deep breath.

In retrospect, Marypat says that the "avalanche of cri-
ses" her family faced forced her to get real with God. "It
wasn't like I would do something like vacuuming and say

six Hail Marys. I would vacuum and say, 'OK, Lord, I need serious help here! How are we going to get through... (name the crisis of the moment).'" Our Lord, it seemed, sent Saint Thérèse armed with a strong dose of fortitude. According to the Catechism of the Catholic Church, "the virtue of fortitude enables one to conquer fear, even fear of death, and to face trials and persecutions. It disposes one even to renounce and sacrifice his life in defense of a just cause" (CCC 1808).

This virtue, full of strength and perseverance, is available to everyone. All we have to do is surrender and ask for it. Fortitude empowered Marypat and her family to embrace Brian wholeheartedly in the midst of grief and sorrow. Fortitude prompted Marypat to plead with the pastor for Brian's acceptance to the neighborhood school. Fortitude energized Marypat as she insisted on an audience with the high school headmaster, knowing full well her case was shaky. And Saint Thérèse brought Marypat fortitude with the sign of a red rose on a door knob, encouraging her to pursue the college that ended up being very well suited for Brian.

Souls with fortitude have conquered their fears out of love. For that reason, fortitude is not a comfortable virtue. Marypat, for example, was anxious and worried about decisions regarding Brian's assimilation into the family, his education, and the accompanying financial challenge. She could have hidden from her fears, settling for less than the best for Brian because of timidity. On the other hand, she might have reacted rashly, alienating school administrators with foolhardy pushiness, for example. However, by surrendering to God in prayer out of love for Brian, Marypat opened her heart to grace in the form of supernatural courage, or fortitude, and the Lord's mission for Brian was accomplished.

Because the college years can be a time of painful transition for mothers, reliance on God, especially through regular daily prayer, avails us of fortitude in the face of our grief or fear. We also build the virtue of fortitude every time we master a new skill, exercise patience (behind the wheel of a car, in line at the grocery store, bearing with a colleague at work), or postpone gratification (amazon.com can make this difficult). We need not wait for a major crisis to ask for this grace. Pope Francis has this advice: "For most of us, the gift of fortitude is exercised in our patient pursuit of holiness in the circumstances of our daily lives. Whenever we feel weary or discouraged along the journey of faith, let us ask the Holy Spirit to grant us the gift of fortitude, to refresh us and to guide our steps with renewed enthusiasm."[35]

---

35 General Audience, by Pope Francis, Vatican City, Italy, May 14, 2014.

Prayer

Almighty Father, I praise you for your strength and might! Raising adult children, especially through the college years, calls for more power and might than I have. I am grateful to have such a strong and loving Father watching over me and my child _____. Please grant me, and all Praying College Moms, the gift of Fortitude. Help me to fight my fears, not with cowardice, but with supernatural courage. I will not run from my troubles but will face them with grace-infused fortitude. Protect me also, Lord, from the other extreme, which is overreacting, rash behavior, or rudeness, stemming from my fears. I surrender to Your strength and count on the grace to live Fortitude whenever life's circumstances require it.

Questions for Reflection:

When my emotions get the best of me, where do I habitually turn for reinforcement and why? To a friend? To a glass of wine? To the television? All of these? To prayer?

Pope Francis says fortitude is often exercised in the ordinary circumstances of daily life. What kinds of ordinary situations in my daily life tempt me to rashness or timidity? What can I do about it?

Prayer Intentions:

Answered Prayers:

Prayer Practice:
When the ordinary things in life feel overwhelming, I will take a deep breath and say a prayer for fortitude, surrendering to God control over everything.

Lord, how can I love you more today than I did yesterday?

My strength and my refuge is the Lord, and he has become my savior. Exodus 15:2

Lord, how can I love you more today than I did yesterday?

Even though I walk through the valley of the shadow of death, I will fear no evil, for you are with me; your rod and your staff comfort me. Psalm 23:4

Lord, how can I love you more today than I did yesterday?

But evils surround me until they cannot be counted. My sins overtake me, so that I can no longer see. They are more numerous than the hairs of my head; my courage fails me. Lord, graciously rescue me! Come quickly to help me, Lord! Psalm 40:13-14

Lord, how can I love you more today than I did yesterday?

Living is the spirit of those who fear the Lord, for their hope is in their savior. Whoever fear the Lord are afraid of nothing and are never discouraged, for he is their hope. Sirach 34:14-16

CHAPTER 6

HIGH FINANCE

WHETHER OUTRAGED, STUPEFIED, or begrudgingly acquiescent, many parents of young adults write six-figure checks for college tuition, room and board—a financial burden that feels, as my husband says, "like driving a Lexus off a cliff." We all know that the cost of college education rises each year, and much has been written about economical alternatives to four-year institutions, financial aid packages, and availability of unique scholarship opportunities.[36] Regardless of a family's monetary wherewithal, college is a serious investment—for many, the largest investment they'll ever make. To finance this undertaking, a prudent parent exercises stewardship; a virtue that balances foresight and responsible planning with healthy detachment and trust in God.[37]

---

36 Underwater Photography Grant, New Look Laser Tattoo Removal Scholarship, National Cartoonist Scholarship, Vegetarian Resource Group Scholarship courtesy of "The Weirdest College Scholarships website, accessed March 17, 2017, http://www.fastweb.com/college-scholarships/articles/the-weirdest-scholarships.

37 Stewardship is a virtue that helps an individual "spend" their time, talent *and* treasure for the glory of God. We are applying stewardship to treasure for this chapter about paying for college.

Cathy and her husband began to save for college from the moment their quadruplets were born. "We knew it was going to be a huge expense all at once so we saved like crazy," she said. Over the years, the family sacrificed by avoiding expensive vacations and home improvements so as to prioritize education. Despite their best efforts, however, when the time came to send all four young adults to college, "we suffered from major sticker shock," Cathy said. The quadruplets were made aware the family's financial shortfall and each contributed according to his or her ability. Two took part-time jobs during school. One was given an academic scholarship which enabled her to go to school out of state. One did a bridge program, attending a community college for the first year, and then transferring the four-year university he had set his sights upon. Now within weeks of celebrating their final graduation, Cathy attributes their ability to pay four college tuitions to working together and "praying about it every single solitary day." As good stewards of their financial resources, the family anticipated their expenses well, saved wisely, and left the rest in God's hands.

Stewardship can guide us, not only in how we prepare to pay the *big* college bills, but in how we teach our children to manage finances during college. "Parents are the number one influence on their children's financial behaviors, so it's up to us to raise a generation of mindful consumers, investors, savers, and givers," says Beth Kobliner, who spearheaded the creation of *Money as You*

Grow, which offers age-appropriate money lessons for children.[38] Although the council is secular, Kobliner's advice incorporates many aspects of Christian Stewardship. She advises teaching children to set up "saving," "spending," and "sharing" jars from an early age. She recommends helping them set age-appropriate financial goals for saving and spending as they enter their teens. When deciding on college, Kobliner says parents should be honest about what the family can afford from the very beginning, and calculate the overall costs (tuition, books, and living expenses) thoroughly before making a final decision.[39]

Carolyn and her husband began planning for their oldest child Katie's college years when Katie entered kindergarten. Now nearly sixteen, Katie has saved the money from summer jobs for her own spending needs. "If she goes out with friends, she no longer asks us for money," Carolyn says. This summer, Carolyn plans to help Katie open a bank account and learn to manage credit. Katie will also begin paying for her cellphone or her car insurance, "get a sense of how much real life can cost," Carolyn says. With this training, Carolyn and her husband hope that Katie will be well prepared to manage college

---

38   Laura Shin, "The 5 Most Important Money Lessons To Teach Your Kids," *Forbes,* October 15, 2013, accessed March 17, 2017, https://www. forbes.com/sites/laurashin/2013/10/15/the-5-most-important-money-lessons-to-teach-your-kids/#a3517f868269. Beth Kobliner's full title includes author of *Get a Financial Life,* and a member of the President's Advisory Council on Financial Capability.

39   Ibid.

spending as a good steward of the gift of education her parents plan to give her.

Should your college students pay for their books? Should they get an allowance for incidentals? Will they be on the meal plan or buy groceries and cook? Will they have a car on campus with those associated costs? Christian parents bring a spiritual dimension to these very practical questions. As stewards of limited financial resources, we embrace with gratitude the means we have, recognizing that every good gift comes from God. We pray for guidance about if and/or how much our young students should contribute to college costs. We allot our resources proportionate to our capability and our discernment. We share the details with them — what's," they "whys," and the "how much"—so that they, too, can be good stewards of what they've received whenever they spend on campus. Finally, we require proper accountability, as the Lord teaches in the parable of the Talents (Matthew 25:14-30).

YOU SPENT WHAT?

All money talk—how it's saved, how it's spent, how it's shared—can be a "hot-button" topic for families, rife with potential for misunderstanding. Holding young adults accountable to their budgets calls for a prayerful and discerning spirit.

"We had the talk and it went well," my friend Tracy told, obviously relieved. "I was really mad about it, but I waited until she was home for the weekend and we could sit down together," she said. Tracy's youngest daughter, Claire, a college junior, had been overspending on the credit card. Claire had been given the card to purchase gas for the car—that was the original plan anyway. Over time, however, Tracy had correctly surmised that her daughter had been hanging out with friends and joining them in activities with little thought to expense. Ubering while on a trip to New York City was the tipping point, Tracy said. "Claire didn't realize that those costs add up, nor did she consider the cheaper option—the subway. It was a parenting problem to me. I needed to teach her to properly understand the value of a dollar," Tracy explained. A "financial intervention" put an end to the spending in the most productive way, Tracy said, by calmly talking it through. "I told her that, in a short period of time, she'd be on her own making her own financial decisions. Having the credit card was not helping her learn. I took the card and gave her enough cash to make it through the end of the year so she'd have to budget," Tracy said. This year, says Tracey, Claire decided on her own to skip the trip to New York because it was "too expensive."

A NO-JUDGMENT ZONE

The economic disparity among students at college can be startling, especially at large state universities with thousands of enrollees. "There are students who have tuition, room, and board paid for and want to go abroad for a semester, plan spring break trips, and travel all summer... and then there are those kids on campus who live in cheap apartments, work three jobs, and access the university food pantry for their meals,"observed one campus administrator. The incongruence is sadly unjust from an objective standpoint. But spiritually speaking, who can say? What's in the heart, not the wallet, matters most to the Lord. "You cannot serve God and mammon," Jesus warns in Matthew 6:26.

Stewardship dictates that, with gratitude we live within our financial means, not striving to "keep up with the Jones" nor nagging our children over every dime they spend. The criteria for our spending (and our giving) is spiritual detachment. Hoarding, stinginess, selfish "give-me's" are symptoms of attachment to material goods. So are eye-rolling judgment and envy of others. What's our cure? When we approach Our Lord in prayer and ask Him how best to spend our money, He advises us! The Rich Young Man encountered Jesus who told him, "You are lacking one thing. Go, sell what you have, and give to [the] poor and you will have treasure in heaven; then come, follow me." (Mark 10:21) When Zacchaeus climbed down from the Sycamore tree full of repentance, Jesus permitted him to keep some of his money. "Behold, half of my possessions, Lord, I shall give to the poor, and if I have extorted anything from anyone I shall repay it four times over"(Luke 19:8). Jesus knew what was best for each soul and acted accordingly.

Likewise, Jesus looks deeply into our hearts and offers us freedom from material attachments by living the virtue of stewardship. When we have approached God with our budget, whether meager or grand, and have accounted for tithing (charitable giving) and thoughtful spending, we can be confident that we have become good stewards of our God-given treasures.

Prayer

God, Father of every good gift, thank You for the financial resources You have given to my family over the years. In good times and in bad, I acknowledge that You are the source of my financial security.

Help our family to be a good steward of Your gifts. Please give us the grace to discern well through prayer how to spend, save, and give according to Your will and for Your glory. I want to spend prudently, save wisely, and give generously.

Since stewardship incorporates time and talent, as well as my "treasure," I humbly ask, Father, that you show me Your will in these areas as well. Amen.

Questions for Reflection:

How do I communicate spending and saving values to my family? Do my actions and words reflect the intentions of my heart or do financial discussions end in chaos or misunderstanding? How can I improve the tone of "money talk" in my home, if necessary?

Do my college-aged youngs adult abide by the budgets I have set for them at school? If so, why? If not, why?

Prayer Intentions:

Answered Prayers:

Prayer Practice: In an effort to "Seek first the Kingdom of God"(Matthew 6:33), I will prayerfully reassess my personal generosity towards others with my time, my talent, and my treasure, and make adjustments as necessary.

Lord, how can I love you more today than I did yesterday?

"But who am I, and who are my people, that we should have the means to contribute so freely? For everything is from you, and what we give is what we have from you. 1 Chronicles 29:14

Lord, how can I love you more today than I did yesterday?

"He who loves money never has money enough." Ecclesiastes 5:10

Lord, how can I love you more today than I did yesterday?

Do not wear yourself out to gain wealth, cease to be worried about it; When your glance flits to it, it is gone! For assuredly it grows wings, like the eagle that flies toward heaven. Proverbs 23:4-5

Lord, how can I love you more today than I did yesterday?

Tell the rich in the present age not to be proud and not to rely on so uncertain a thing as wealth but rather on God, who richly provides us with all things for our enjoyment. Tell them to do good, to be rich in good works, to be generous, ready to share, thus accumulating as treasure a good foundation for the future, so as to win the life that is true life. 1 Timothy 6:17-19

CHAPTER 7

WRITING STRAIGHT WITH CROOKED LINES

IF YOU HAD a smidgen of pixie dust or a magic wand, what kind of academic future would you conjure up for your college student? Perhaps he would be accepted to Harvard or Stanford, with a full merit-based scholarship. Or, she would win the high school science award and earn a place of honor at MIT? Or the twins would dance so well that the Juilliard School would plead to admit them. Regardless of the specifics, most parents would imagine a no-cost, four-year degree, concluding with a summa cum laude award ceremony, featuring a happy graduate, well prepared for the future. Waving a magic wand can satiate the imagination but a future plotted out in our own reality can twist, turn, zig, and zag until we are so disoriented that we make a fatal mistake...We rely on our own strength! God Our Father is a creative genius, and only He can write straight with crooked lines.

Katie chose a college with a lot of familial connections that wasn't too far from home, which made her mother happy. The school had name recognition, a solid reputation, and a Catholic identity. As the oldest, she was determined to make her family proud over the next four years. Everything changed when she arrived on campus.

"I don't understand why people put a bunch of eighteen-year-olds in one place, and expect them to behave," Katie says of her freshman year experience. "I was very cognizant going into college that there would not be as much support for my morals as I was used to, but I thought that nothing would challenge me so much that I would break. I was way overconfident. I started to see awful things right away," she said.

The campus, which was located in the center of a large metropolis, shielded the students from urban dangers like nearby gang activity, but Katie felt that "...it was always kind of a dangerous environment." The school reported three times as many sexual assaults than at other similar institutions during her years there, Katie said. There were bar fights and altercations between students of different ethnicities, she said. "I was on edge a lot of the time," she added.

Katie began to date midway through her freshman year, but the relationship was short lived. "After three months, he said he was breaking up with me because I wouldn't sleep with him and he began dating the girl the next dorm over," she said. The rejection hurt less than the attitude of her girlfriends, Katie said. "Instead of supporting me, some of them encouraged me to compromise or give in to him," she said. "And then, one by one by one, they all gave in saying 'Whatever' or 'It's fine,'" Katie said. "It was totally demoralizing to watch."

Katie says she could have stayed, but, by sophomore year she was asking herself, "Why am I spending every day fighting against all of this?" If she transferred, Katie would be swapping the prestige of a nationally ranked institution for a lesser-known school. When she talked to her parents, they supported her wholeheartedly and the transfer happened quickly over Christmas break of her Sophomore year.

The new environment was safe, the curriculum was solidly Catholic, and her friends supported her resolve to live chastely. Katie loved it immediately. "Right now, I could have drinks with any one of five hundred people from school and enjoy myself," she said of her new friends. "They're like-minded, caring, and faithful, which is such a nice difference. They asked me, 'Who wants to go to Mass today?'" Katie said. "This school, with its tight knit community, may not be for everyone, but it was just right for me," she said. Katie graduated and now works as a journalist.

Katie transferred for moral encouragement, but Kevin postponed college altogether for emotional reasons. "I just didn't feel ready for college when it came time to go," Kevin said. "Most kids were excited about getting away and partying and that wasn't appealing to me at all. And I wasn't very responsible about my school work. So if I wasn't going to do the work and wasn't into partying, it was just going to be a waste of money," he explained. His parents and friends frequently offered their "two cents" about the importance of a college degree, Kevin said, but instead, he worked construction and then took a nine-to-five job in residential real estate. For nearly three years, he worked while his friends finished college.

Over time, Kevin began to realize that schooling might improve his business prospects. "I started to think a degree would give me more credibility among certain kinds of real estate clients," he explained. At the same time, a good friend of the family talked "man-to-man" with Kevin about going to school. "The timing was everything. I was ready to listen," Kevin said. Kevin now treats school like his job. "When I don't have classes, I get up and study," he said. "I want to finish quickly, but I'm not going to compromise on my grades," he added. Kevin plans to study year-round while working part-time and should graduate in three years.

Nelly, now a mother and grandmother, jokes that "my son majored in universities and my daughter majored in majors." Years ago, when Nelly's son went far away to college, "I remember how my heart was wrenched," she recalled. Her sorrow didn't last too long because, after the second semester, he transferred to a local university and then to another...Nelly's daughter also took a circuitous route, studying for years accumulating courses without a degree in mind. They both graduated eventually and Nelly now chuckles about it. "Back then, we didn't think it was very funny, but now I see how the best plans can get waylaid by a fork or two in the road. We all somehow got through," she said.

Not all young adults "get through" nor do some even go to college. They enlist in the military, start a business, go to trade or vocational school, or volunteer, foregoing the traditional four-year college option. Whenever life veers out the confines we imagined, it's easy to forget that Our Father is near, and He loves us and our children more than we do. God expresses His infinite love for us through the actions of His Divine Providence. "Creation has its own goodness and proper perfection, but it did not spring forth complete from the hands of the Creator. The universe was created 'in a state of journeying' (*in statu viae*) toward an ultimate perfection yet to be attained, to which God has destined it. We call 'divine providence' the dispositions by which God guides his creation toward this perfection" (CCC 302).

In His Divine Providence, God assures us of His temporal help and all the grace we need to manage life's twists and turns to reach eternal salvation. What does temporal help from God look like? For women of faith, coincidences are "God-incidences." Perfect timing is "God's timing." A unexpected college acceptance is "miraculous." News of financial aid is a "Godsend." A failure is an opportunity to let God be our strength. When our college-aged young adults stray from path *we* planned for them, we cling to God's Divine Providence, knowing, as Jesus tells us, that our loving Father is in ultimate control of our lives and can be trusted with everything. "Are not two sparrows sold for a small coin?" Jesus says, "Yet not one of them falls to the ground without your Father's knowledge. Even all the hairs of your head are counted. So do not be afraid; you are worth more than many sparrows" (Matthew 10:29-32). As time passes, we one day, like Nelly, chuckle at these days, relishing the good we now see was God in action.

OUR PART

Divine Providence is mysteriously all-encompassing, but it does not liberate us from cooperating with God's movements in our lives. To the contrary, God graciously empowers us to be "coworkers" (1 Corinthians 3:9) through our actions, prayers, and sufferings (CCC 307). We don't always recognize God's invitation to cooperate with Him because faith may require us to jump into a scary void without any immediate assurance of God's presence. We blindly acquiesce, for example, when our child transfers from one college to another unexpectedly. We pray and gently nudge him when he decides to postpone college for what seems like forever. And we suffer through moments, or even years of darkness and confusion, until one day we bow low before the Divine Providence of God, realizing He was there the whole time.

The next time we're tempted to wave a wand to rewrite the future our son or daughter seems to have chosen, let's remember that all genuine power rests in God alone. With prayerful actions, intercession, and the merits of our suffering as parents, we can rely on His Divine Providence to bring us all, as the Catechism says, to our ultimate perfection, straightening every crooked turn we take!

"In all your ways acknowledge him, and he will make straight your paths." (Proverbs 3:6)

Dear Father, Son and Holy Spirit, triune God, Creator, and Deliverer, through your Divine Providence you work all things for good for those who love You (Romans 8:28). I praise You and acknowledge Your sovereignty in my life and over my child _____. I want to

- surrender my dreams for _____ to You, Lord,
- give over my expectations of _____ to You, Lord,
- trust in your governance when chaos erupts in _____ life,
- and love _____ unconditionally.

Please help me, Father, to work hard to fulfill Your will in my life and for the sake of _____, believing that by cooperating with Your grace, all will be accomplished for your great glory and the salvation of our souls.

Questions for Reflection:
What short- and long-term goals do I have for my college-aged young adult during this time in his life? Does he corroborate these goals? What concrete things can I do to help him achieve his goals?

God enlivens our weak faith when we exercise it by trusting Him. At times, He strengthens our faith with very tangible answers to prayer. When has God answered my prayer in a surprising way? What characteristics of God are expressed by an answered prayer, and how does that experience invigorate my faith?

Prayer Intentions:

Answered Prayers:

Prayer Practice:
I will watch for little signs of God's Divine Providence in my life this month and offer a little prayer of thanksgiving each time I recognize His action in my day.

Lord, how can I love you more today than I did yesterday?

Therefore every loyal person should pray to you in time of distress. Though flood waters threaten, they will never reach him. You are my shelter; you guard me from distress; with joyful shouts of deliverance you surround me. Psalm 32:6-7

Lord, how can I love you more today than I did yesterday?

Life and love you granted me, and your providence has preserved my spirit. Job 10:12

Lord, how can I love you more today than I did yesterday?

...for you have furnished even in the sea a road, and through the waves a steady path, showing that you can save from any danger, so that even one without skill may embark. Wisdom 14:3-4

Lord, how can I love you more today than I did yesterday?

Where can I go from your spirit? From your presence, where can I flee? If I ascend to the heavens, you are here; if I lie down in Sheol, there you are. If I take the wings of dawn and dwell beyond the sea, Even there your hand guides me, your right hand holds me fast. Psalm 139:7-10

CHAPTER 8

SHALT THOU NOT DRINK?

EMMA'S PARENTS RAISED her with a strong faith, in a loving, stable family. Her faith was nurtured as she attended CCD and later taught side by side with her mother. Although her father was Jewish, he unwaveringly endorsed the raising of their children in the Catholic faith, and Emma felt his strong support. When the time came, Emma enrolled in a state university in the South to study elementary education, inspired by her experience teaching CCD. She left home with the confidence that her parents and God loved her very much. Apparently, this foundation wasn't sufficient enough to protect her from the dangers of over-drinking when she became immersed in the social environment at school.

Within days of her arrival at college, Emma said she had made the following "shocking observations."

- Everyone called themselves Christians, but it seemed that no one went to church. No one was active in their faith.
- The college atmosphere seemed very liberal.

- Everyone drank alcohol, and many smoked marijuana.
- Casual sex seemed to be the norm.

By the second semester of her freshman year, Emma had succumbed to her surroundings. Drinking heavily one night, she slept with a young man she had just met. "I knew sex was sacred and to be kept for marriage. It was not supposed to happen," she said. "But, I had seen my friends…some of them had told me to just get it over with. So I threw away everything I had learned about my faith for a one night thing."

Drinking, dating, and partying every weekend, Emma still went to church once in a while and volunteered for a Christian group on campus. "I was going through the motions of faith—doing what I'd always done—while I tried to figure out who I was," she said.

Emma came close to despair one night when she saw "the guy" at a party. "I felt a wave of guilt that sent me into a tailspin," she said. "That night, I came back to my dorm and lay on the floor and cried. I tried to pray, telling God I was done…tired of searching for happiness in all the wrong places. No more boys…no more drinking…I was a mess. I knew that if I kept it all up, things would end poorly, and I needed to turn my life around." Despite her frenetic emotional state, Emma says she realized God was present. "He was there, and I felt He would forgive me," she said. "I still need to forgive myself."

Emma didn't have to wait long for goodness to enter her life. The next day, an upperclassman named Pete, whom Emma had met briefly weeks before, sent her a text asking to meet for coffee. Pete was a junior and an officer in the Christian fraternity on campus. Under the rules of his fraternity, members do not drink or engage in premarital sex. "I feel lucky he is Catholic, because there are so few Catholics in the South," said Emma. "We're both young and have things we're working out, but we're doing it together," she said. "He's my first real boyfriend, and I respect Pete. I didn't respect the other guys I dated."

Meeting Pete helped Emma make up her mind to return to her faith, but he's not the only reason she's living differently. "It's tough to see everyone partying and know that that's not something I need to be doing. My freshman roommate is still drinking and being crazy, and she's right next door in the dorm. But I'm on a different path now. I know who I am when I'm drunk, and it's not someone I want to be."

"Drinking at college has become a ritual that students often see as an integral part of their higher education experience," according to the National Institute on Alcohol Abuse and Alcoholism.[40] The majority of college students drink, and the vast majority of those who

---

40   National Institute on Alcohol Abuse and Alcoholism College Fact Sheet.

drink binge, NIAAA reported a national study in 2014.[41] The consequences for students who abuse alcohol can be deadly.

Researchers estimate that each year:

- **Death:** About 1,825 college students between the ages
- of eighteen and twenty-four die from alcohol-related unintentional injuries, including motor-vehicle crashes.
- **Assault:** About 696,000 students between the ages of eighteen and twenty-four are assaulted by another student who has been drinking.
- **Sexual Assault:** About 97,000 students between the ages of eighteen and twenty-four report experiencing alcohol-related sexual assault or date rape.
- **Academic Problems:** About one in four college students report academic consequences from drinking, including missing class, falling behind in class, doing poorly on exams or papers, and receiving lower grades overall.[42]

Few of us doubt that alcohol abuse on campuses poses a significant public health risk, but we parent on the issue

---

41 Ibid.

42 Ibid.

in vastly different ways. Aware that their children likely drank in high school, some parents give their tacit blessing to college-aged kids who drink. "Hey, these kids are old enough to go to war. They can certainly have a drink or two, or three." Other parents "cross their fingers" and hope for the best because they don't know how to prepare their children to face these pressures on campus. And a third group of parents forbids their children to drink (reminding them that drinking is illegal at their age), and those results are mixed.

Understanding what motivates college students to abuse alcohol can be an important first step in persuading under aged adults not to drink. When they arrive on campus, college students mix with hundreds or thousands of strangers, resulting in a uniquely complex situation fraught with social anxiety. More than 75 percent of college students admit that they drink to quell this anxiety.[43] Alcohol is also an integral part of many long-standing collegiate sports traditions, like pre-gaming in dorms and tailgating at sports arena parking lots. Administrations, alumni, and students can be reluctant to abandon these rituals. Greek life can also promote heavy drinking,

---

43   Robert Yagoda,"College Students and Binge Drinking: When a Rite of Passage Becomes a Path to Destruction," US News and World Report, November 9, 2016, accessed November 14, 2016, http://health.usnews.com/health-care/for-better/articles/2016-11-09/college-students-and-binge-drinking-when-a-rite-of-passage-becomes-a-path-to-destruction. Accessed November 14, 2016.

although, as Pete's choice illustrates, not all sororities or fraternities do.[44]

ONE PARENT'S COLLEGE ORIENTATION PROGRAM

Shopping "back to school" specials, loading the car, or setting up the dorm room does not adequately prepare your freshman for his/her first weeks of school in the alcohol-laden environment on most college campuses. These young adults need praying parents, a strong moral foundation, and some well-timed words of advice to resist these ever-present temptations.

Mike and his wife equip their college-aged students with what Mike calls a coherent philosophy of life years before they go to school. "They know that we think they are unique and special, that they have an irreplaceable mission from God, that God loves them, and they can trust God with anything. When they screw up, and they're going to screw up, God is there for them and so are we," Mike says.

Mike, his wife, and their extended family drink socially in their home where alcohol is not treated as the "forbidden fruit." The children are sometimes poured a thimble full of wine during the family meal, and as they

---

44 National Institute on Alcohol Abuse and Alcoholism College Fact Sheet. http://pubs.niaaa.nih.gov/publications/CollegeFactSheet/College FactSheet.pdf

grow up, they are invited to join the adults drinking wine around the dinner table.

Mike wants to help his children develop a mature relationship with alcohol that will serve them through their adult life. He believes that they must learn to avoid situations where alcohol can lead to trouble, especially during those heady early days of college.

Mike recognizes, as do many parents, that college drinking on college campuses is dangerous, and often illegal, and that during the first six weeks of freshman year students are particularly vulnerable to peer pressure. Before his children leave for school, Mike sits down with each one for an "orientation" of his own design. The topic of alcohol is addressed in the context of the personal responsibility each has to make the most of school. First, he reminds them that college is a privilege others have worked hard to give them. He reminds them that studying is their job for the next four years, and if they do well, it can set them up for the rest of their life. Mike then paints a visual picture of what they are likely to encounter. "You're going to see really outrageous things, and I want you to see them sober," he says. "I want you to have a good time, but I am asking, as your father, that you do not have a drop of alcohol for the first six weeks."

"You don't trust me?"

"Of course I don't," Mike responds. He reminds them that everyone is "deeply flawed" and that self-sufficiency "is a myth." One beer can easily lead to two, "and we don't know what we're really capable of when we're 'half in the bag,'" he says. With a mixture of humor and candid illustrations, Mike then goes through practical scenarios with them, and together they work out strategies for keeping the six-week pledge and remaining sober thereafter.

Have Mike's kids kept their pledge? Yes. Much later, they have acknowledged that they did indeed see "outrageous things"—enough to convince them that getting drunk isn't cool at all.

IS DRUNKENNESS A SIN?

Mike's approach to college drinking is practical, and more importantly, persuasive. He gets results without dwelling directly on the sinful nature of drunkenness. However, it's important to note that drunkenness is a sin—one that separates us from God permanently if not repented of, according to Saint Paul. "Now the works of the flesh are obvious: immorality, impurity, licentiousness, idolatry, sorcery, hatreds, rivalry, jealousy, outbursts of fury, acts of selfishness, dissensions, factions, occasions of envy, *drinking bouts*, orgies, and the like. I warn you, as I warned you before, that those who do such things will not inherit the kingdom of God" (Galatians 5:19-21). [emphasis added].

In fact, Scripture has a lot to say about drunkenness. A quick search reveals nearly forty verses of Scripture warning against the "evils of drunkenness." Proverbs 23:29-35 reads as if it was written by an observer at a college frat party:

Who scream? Who shout?
Who have strife? Who have anxiety?
Who have wounds for nothing?
Who have bleary eyes?
Whoever linger long over wine,
    whoever go around quaffing wine.

Do not look on the wine when it is red,
    when it sparkles in the cup.
It goes down smoothly,
    but in the end it bites like a serpent,
    and stings like an adder.

Your eyes behold strange sights,
    and your heart utters incoherent things;
You are like one sleeping on the high seas,
    sprawled at the top of the mast.

"They struck me, but it did not pain me;
    they beat me, but I did not feel it.
When can I get up,
    when can I go out and get more?"

Drunkenness falls under the capital sin of gluttony; a disordered appetite for food or drink. Saint Paul defines the glutton as someone whose God is their belly (Philippians 3:19). "Their end is destruction," he says. "Their glory is in their shame...Their minds are occupied with earthly things" (Philippians 3:18-19).

Binge drinking at college is an obvious sin of gluttony, but children who never take a sip might also be culpable, according to the Catechism 1868:

Sin is a personal act. Moreover, we have a responsibility for the sins committed by others when *we cooperate in them*:

—by participating directly and voluntarily in them;
—by ordering, advising, praising, or approving them;
—by not disclosing or not hindering them when we have an obligation to do so;
—by protecting evil-doers.

Cheering at the beer pong table? Egging on the guys taking shots to celebrate a football win? Standing by while a girlfriend gets drunk, or worse... leaving her behind at a party? Covering up a friend's drunken indiscretions? Comforting the hung over friend with comments like, "Whatever" and "It's OK; everyone does it."

Not many college students are blessed with the moral integrity to abstain from alcohol or refrain from encouraging it, much less proactively oppose it. Our college-aged children need our help, whether they vocalize it or not. "Research shows that students who choose not to drink often do so because their parents discussed alcohol use and its adverse consequences with them."[45] Additionally, drinking is least probable among students who live at home and commute to school,[46] presumably because of ongoing direct accountability to their parents.

PARENTING WITH PRUDENCE

Fighting a temptation to gluttony (in our example, over-drinking) requires the exercise of temperance. A perfectly temperate college student overcomes peer pressure by simply and self-assuredly explaining that he doesn't drink. He moderates his food and alcohol intake in the football stands, at late-night dorm parties, off and on campus-—in every circumstance. His exceptional self-mastery shines as he stands apart from his peers, restraining every appetite for the glory of God. Does that sound like any college student you know?

Desirable as it is, we know that the virtue of temperance is hard to exercise, especially for young adults. Scientific evidence suggests that temperance is difficult because eighteen to twenty-year-olds lack a fully developed pre-frontal cortex, the part of the brain that regulates impulse control. This makes them more likely than others to engage in risky behavior, especially if someone

---

45 Ibid.
46 Ibid.

is watching them.[47] There's not much room in this young psyche for self-control, sobriety, and vigilance...in other words, for temperance.

Temperance defeats the sin of gluttony head-on, but the sister virtue of Prudence might more effectively inspire college students to win the cultural battle against alcohol abuse. Temperance draws on emotional and mental willpower in a moment of temptation, but the prudent person uses reason to conquer vice. The Catechism tells us that "Prudence is 'right reason in action,'" as defined by Saint Thomas Aquinas, following Aristotle (CCC 1806). To evoke prudent decision-making, children are given a thorough understanding of moral principles—not just the "what" but the "why." This "remote preparation" then kicks in when college students face a dilemma. They exercise prudence, acknowledging its obvious merits by weighing the pros and cons of getting drunk, and concluding rightly to stay sober. In other words, they "apply these moral principles to particular cases without error and overcome doubts about the good to achieve and the evil to avoid" (CCC 1806).

Mike hopes that, by telling his children about the dangers of drunkenness—possible arrest, unplanned sexual encounters, hangovers, etc.—and by making his expectations very clear, they will see enough evidence in the first

---

47   Sandra Aamodt, "Brain Maturity Extends Well Beyond the Teen Years," interviewed by Brian Candy, NPR, October 10, 2011.

six weeks to convince them not to put themselves at risk in that way. In effect, he hopes that they are empowered by his moral teachings and their own observations to exercise prudence when the time comes: to discern how to drink responsibly. It has worked for them. How do you talk to your college students about alcohol? Do you discuss the destructive consequences of drunkenness? What about its sinfulness? You know the best way to approach your child, and prudence dictates that you must! Since college students fare better if their parents discuss alcohol use with them, how much better prepared are those whose parents have prayed to God for prudence, and in that same Spirit, offer their loving support and guidance?

Prayer

Dear Father, Creator of every good thing, Your Son made wine from water. Alcohol is a gift and blessing—one that requires virtue to enjoy. I ask you as a praying college mom to bless _____ and help her resist the temptation to drink alcohol at school. Bless her with the gift of Prudence so that she can make wise decisions in every circumstance. Give her courage and strength to stand apart from those who live the status quo in social situations on campus. May she be a sober, light-filled, genuine friend to others. Allow her to radiate your love, so that she is a good example of virtue and brings glory to You. And if she falls, Lord, forgive her! And bless me with the grace to help reorient her in a spirit of love, not judgment, so that she can learn to lean on You the way I do, knowing that You are trustworthy and Good.

Questions for Reflection:

What is my family's attitude about drinking alcohol? How do I feel about college-aged drinking in general? How does my outlook contribute to my child's inclination to drink on campus, or strengthen her to resist?

Saint Paul says that drunkenness is a sin—one that separates us from God. Is getting tipsy sinful? What about "accidental" drunkenness? Alcoholism? What are the criteria for mortal sin? For a thorough explanation from the Catechism about mortal sin, see Appendix 4.

Prayer Intentions:

Answered Prayers:

Prayer Practice:
I will pray for the gift of Prudence for myself, my husband, and my college student(s) every morning during this next month, listening for inspiration about when to talk to him/her about alcohol and what to say.

Lord, how can I love you more today than I did yesterday?

Therefore I prayed, and prudence was given me; I pleaded and the spirit of Wisdom came to me. King Solomon speaking in Wisdom 7:7

Lord, how can I love you more today than I did yesterday?

Do not try to prove your strength by wine-drinking, for wine has destroyed many. Sirach 31:25 (NRSCV)

Lord, how can I love you more today than I did yesterday?

A fool rejects his father's discipline, But he who regards reproof is sensible. Proverbs 15:5

Lord, how can I love you more today than I did yesterday?

So whether you eat or drink, or whatever you do, do everything for the glory of God. 1Corinthians 10:31

CHAPTER 9

COLLEGE? OR NOT...

LIVING IN A suburb where nearly every child goes to college, Ellen navigated the typical conversation starters with some trepidation: "How are your kids doing? How old are they now? Oh, wonderful...where do they go to school?" It was challenging to offer a response that did not reveal too much personal information about her daughter Anna's life, yet addressed the question head-on. The simple truth: the twenty-year-old had withdrawn from community college—for the second time—and her future college enrollment was uncertain. Ellen, who counsels students preparing for college, knows very well that not everyone graduates in four years, and that some don't graduate at all, "but it feels so different, when it's your own child," she said. Is Ellen despondent? Angry? Frustrated? Or even embarrassed? Surprisingly not. "Last Tuesday, I came out of the chapel with the most remarkable peace," said Ellen. "I was almost levitating," she joked.

Ellen's peace is of the supernatural variety—a peace "surpassing all understanding" (Philippians 4:7), borne of her fidelity to prayer. Jesus first gave this peace to his

125

disciples immediately after His resurrection. "Peace I leave with you; my peace I give to you. Not as the world gives do I give it to you. Do not let your hearts be troubled or afraid" (John 14:27). His peace is a gift given to souls who draw close to receive it. Yet, when we're anxious or afraid, the last person we tend to trust is the one who can fix everything: Jesus.

Seventeen years ago, Ellen's faith was shaken when doctors confirmed that Anna had juvenile diabetes. A later diagnosis of celiac disease complicated Anna's dietary regimen and probably contributed to the deterioration of her mental and physical health. When Anna went from a happy eighth grader to a depressed high schooler and eventually dropped out altogether, "life became torturous," Ellen said. "I even questioned the use of praying," Ellen said. "We saw doctors, we worked with the school, we would try to be with our other two younger kids, but it was one disappointing, discouraging thing after another," she said. "I subconsciously took the attitude with God that, since He didn't seem to be responding to my prayers, He must be off doing His own thing."

Meanwhile, Anna spent difficult days that turned into months getting a GED[48] and taking the SAT to prepare for college, while working part-time. She was not managing her illnesses well, which caused a tremendous strain on the family. At wit's end, Ellen eventually drew

---

48   General Education Development, a high-school certification.

inspiration from her husband who attended daily Mass and visited Jesus in the Blessed Sacrament at the parish Adoration chapel. "I wasn't very good at getting there, but one Sunday at Mass, as I was thinking about it, the pastor invited people to sign up for specific hours before the Blessed Sacrament," Ellen said. She signed up for one hour weekly.

The time Ellen spent with Jesus in Adoration didn't bring her peace instantaneously. "I was so distracted at Adoration that I was becoming discouraged. I started feeling that I haven't been as good a person as I could have been and I felt a little like what was going on with Anna was my fault," she explained. The Catechism teaches that distraction is a "habitual difficulty in prayer. To set about hunting down distractions would be to fall into their trap, when all that is necessary is to turn back to our heart..." (CCC 2729).

Our Lord intervened, sending Ellen a spiritual companion for her holy hours in the person of Father Jacque Philippe. "I've read all his books," Ellen said, "but the most helpful has been *Searching for and Maintaining Peace*." Father Philippe's writings "hold you to account but don't beat you down," she said. "Through Saint Thérése of Lisieux and Saint Teresa of Avila, who are often quoted, I began to understand that I was making myself too big in all of this. In a beautiful way, I started to realize my littleness and to trust...fully trust...in God's love for me and for my children. I slowly began to become more peaceful even though our outward circumstances had not markedly changed," she said.

At Adoration, Ellen says she often feels as if God is talking directly to her. Last Tuesday, she was especially consoled when she read from a chapter on confronting the sufferings of those close to us. "One thing is certain: God loves our dear ones infinitely more than we do, and infinitely better. He wants us to believe in this love, and also to know how to entrust those who are dear to us into His hands. And this will often be a much more efficacious way of helping them."[49]

The peace that Ellen now feels has positively impacted her home life and her relationship with Anna. "I approach Anna differently these days. She is much more inclined to hear what I have to say if I'm not agitated. And, I'm not as frustrated, thinking that I can change things by myself. This is good for both of us," said Ellen.

Anna's life is still not unfolding the way Ellen would choose for her, but Ellen draws spiritual consolation from two recent developments. Anna agreed to enroll in a trial which requires wearing a continuous glucose monitor. Ellen hopes it will help Anna manage her blood sugar levels more efficiently. While she was at the office, Anna met a nurse who convinced her to follow a gluten-free diet to address her celiac disease, finally. "I had told her all of

---

49   Jacques Philippe, *Searching for and Maintaining Peace: A Small Treatise on Peace of Heart* (New York: Alba House, 2002), 48.

this before, but this time she listened," Ellen said. "These little glimmers of hope for her physical well-being have been so uplifting to us! I consider them tangible answers to prayer."

Ellen acknowledges that prayer has also helped her appreciate God's perfect timing in her life. "I'm growing in my faith—maybe later than I would have liked—but I believe I am reading these books at a time when I really need them. They really set me straight, reminding me that I need to let go." Ellen now knows that God is not, "off doing His own thing." Instead, God is helping her to trust in His plan for Anna and for the whole family. "I don't have the same sadness about Anna's future. Whatever happens, God is with us. He has always been with us."

Prayer

God my Father, You are the source of all peace. Your Son, our Lord Jesus Christ is the Prince of peace. Our Blessed Mother, Mary, is the Queen of Peace. You mention "peace" in the Scriptures more than four hundred times. Through the Holy Spirit, I receive the fruit of peace. As Jesus brought the gift of peace to His disciples on the eve of His resurrection, I ask you Father for this same gift. Shower me, my child _____ and my whole family with Your peace.

> When I am distracted in prayer, be my peace, Lord.
> Help me to be faithful to my time of prayer.
> When I am worried about my child _____, be my peace, Lord.
> When I dwell on past circumstances, be my peace, Lord.
> When I fret about the future, be my peace, Lord.
> When I resist surrendering to You and try to control things, be my peace, Lord.
> When I worry about what others think, be my peace, Lord.

Lord, you know better than I do how I need Your peace. I trust in You and praise Your name. Amen.

Questions for Reflection:

Peace is a fruit of the Holy Spirit. What spiritual dispositions, thoughts, or attitudes promote peace in a soul? Conversely, identify some dispositions that wreak havoc with peace in the soul. What is their origin?

Prayer Intentions:

Answered Prayers:

Prayer Practice:

What has caused me to worry in the last twenty-four to forty-eight hours? (Make a list of each circumstance—big or small.) Read over the list, adding each "worry" to the prayer above, followed by, be my peace, Lord. Pray the prayer and repeat as necessary.

Lord, how can I love you more today than I did yesterday?

"Permit me to formulate an axiom that is a little paradoxical: Above all we must never lose our peace because we can never find or be as much at peace as we would like! Our reeducation is long and it is necessary to have a lot of patience with ourselves." Searching for and Maintaining Peace, p. 81.

Lord, how can I love you more today than I did yesterday?

"When we are powerless, let us be quiet and let God act. How many people lose their peace because they want, at any price, to change those around them!" Searching for and Maintaining Peace, p. 55.

Lord, how can I love you more today than I did yesterday?

"God may allow me to occasionally lack money, health, abilities and virtues, but He will never leave me in want of Himself, of His assistance and His mercy or of anything that would allow me to grow unceasingly ever closer to Him, to love Him more intensely, to better love my neighbor and to achieve holiness." Searching for and Maintaining Peace, p. 45

Lord, how can I love you more today than I did yesterday?

"Let us therefore learn to abandon ourselves, to have total confidence in God, in the big things as in the small, with the simplicity of little children." Searching for and Maintaining Peace, p. 35.

CHAPTER 10

NOT HAPPY AND GAY

FOR RYAN, THE four years at his Catholic college were fraught with anxiety, teasing, foiled heterosexual experimentation, and uneasy bonding with the guys in his all-male dorm. He coped by calling home to "talk things out." He also drank alcohol and smoked marijuana. Periodically, he attended group therapy provided by the university to allay his anxiety. He excelled academically and socially. No one suspected he was gay, or if they did, they didn't say so.

Sally told her parents in a letter when she was thirteen years old that she felt differently than other girls, according to her mother. "I am either gay or bi or do not know what. I hope you will accept this," she wrote. Sally's mom was surprised by the letter, felt that Sally was too young to know for sure about these things, and decided to wait and see. "I didn't know what to make of it," Sally's mom said. In high school, Sally had very few close friends. During sophomore year she wore contacts, makeup and mascara. That summer, she shaved her head. By her junior prom, Sally had become vegan, lost weight, and looked beautiful, "like Audrey Hepburn," her mother said. She attended that prom with a gay friend. Just before college started, Sally had a brief summer romance with a young man who thought he was a girl. None of these iterations of personality seemed to work for Sally, according to her mom. Sally finished college and now lives miles away with some "very accepting" friends and her mom is "happy Sally is happy."

Jason experimented with same-sex relationships as a young teen and was "found out" by his mother. Dangerously depressed, Jason visited doctors and psychologists trying to sort things out during those years. He took medication but continued to suffer under the watchful and concerned eye of his doctors and his mother. He withdrew emotionally, sharing very little with his mother, and nothing with his father. The family moved often, and Jason ended up at a college half a continent away from his parents. They didn't hear much from him for a while. After his father's posting concluded, however, Jason's parents were able to move close to his school. "I was so happy to be near Jason again," his mom said, "and he brought some friends over for dinner a couple of times. They were effeminate, although Jason is not." Then, one night, Jason was rushed to the hospital by his friends. He called his mom the next morning to fill her in and let her know he was OK. She raced to see him and found his friends there also. "I was really hurt he didn't think to call me first, especially since we were only fifteen minutes away," she said. "He told me the problem was a stomach ulcer, but I worry that wasn't the truth," she added.

Dave's parents discovered he was gay late one night when he came home in a drunken stupor as a high school junior. Awakened by the dog barking, Dave's mother Julie was surprised to find him crying on the stoop in the freezing cold. Seeing that he was also drunk, she lost her temper and ushered him into the house, waking Dave's father in the process. "What were you doing, and what do you have to say for yourself?" she asked.

"If you really want to know, I just hung up from the suicide prevention hotline because...I am gay," he sobbed. His father immediately engulfed him in a gigantic bear hug and the three of them talked well into the next morning. Slowly he told his siblings, other family members, and close friends.

When the time for college arrived, Dave chose a Catholic school and entered as an openly gay freshman. He pledged a fraternity and the men acknowledged and welcomed their only gay pledge. Dave has graduated from college and lives at home. For now, his mother's chief concern is his not his sexuality but his drinking. When he drinks, he often overdoes it, she says. Dave is now a bit of a homebody, and his mother is grateful for the relative peace in the house.

All of these young people share similar backgrounds: they were born into loving Catholic families, educated at prominent institutions, and are gifted with intelligence and talent. They also share a monumental cross—same-sex attraction and an inability to reconcile it with their faith and their perceived expectations of their parents. Several of them sought relief through Catholicism; one went to daily Mass for a period, another said novenas. Their parents, all practicing Catholics, mourn the loss of a "white picket fence" future for their children and pray for their return to the faith. Outside this microcosm of suffering, how does the rest of the world, in particular this college-aged generation, feel about same-sex attraction?

THE WAYS OF THE WORLD

When Ryan came out shortly after graduating, his parents were devastated but most of his college friends didn't react negatively. Same-sex attraction elicits a "yawn" from millennials on college campuses. The latest studies indicate a similar attitude in the nation at large. According to the Barna Group, between 50 and 79 percent of Americans consider it "very or somewhat extreme" to believe that sexual relationships between people of the same sex are morally wrong.[50] With the Supreme Court's legalization of same-sex marriage in 2016, it seems that those who uphold the Catholic Church teaching on homosexuality

50 "Five Ways Christianity Is Increasingly Viewed as Extremist - Barna Group," February 23, 2016, accessed November 21, 2016, https://www.barna.com/research/five-ways-christianity-is-increasingly-viewed-as-extremist/.

are now a minority in this country. Even the word "homo-sexuality" has been replaced by the culturally applauded all-inclusive term "LGBTQ."[51]

By contrast, the church teaches that a homosexual act is intrinsically wrong. According to the Catechism, "[homosexual acts] are contrary to the natural law. They close the sexual act to the gift of life. They do not pro-ceed from a genuine affective and sexual complementar-ity" (CCC 2357). Homosexuals are called, like all children of God, to live chastely—a lifestyle that resonates with few college-aged hetero- or homosexuals, so steeped are they in modern culture, which aggressively promotes infidelity and fornication through the likes of reality television and online pornography.

Anticipating the need for a cohesive and compelling restatement of church teaching about sex, Saint John Paul II left us *Theology of the Body*, a series of 129 lectures given from 1979 to 1984, which communicate the tran-scendent beauty of human sexuality. This pontificate also bequeathed to us a newly revised Catechism of the Catholic Church, published in 1992. Together, Catholics of all ages have the tools we need to comprehend the church's teaching on sex, and, with the help of grace from the Sacraments, to embrace these natural and supernatu-ral truths, and live them.

---

51 Lesbian, gay, bisexual, transgender, and questioning or queer.

Additionally, the church has provided pastoral support for more than thirty years to those with same-sex attraction and their loved ones through two ministries: EnCourage for families and Courage for the individual. These ministries "promote close Christian friendships as an antidote to the kind of sexual activities that same-sex attracted are urged to adopt as part of the gay scene. Here, they can share their heavy cross with other like-minded Catholics and find the strength to live chastely," says Burman Skrable, a co-coordinator for EnCourage.

AN UPHILL BATTLE

A gay person's desire for intimacy, for a lifelong committed relationship, or for a feeling of belonging is natural to every human, man or woman. Catholicism teaches that the homosexual act is wrong, but that same-sex attraction is *not* a sin. For those with same-sex attraction who want to partake in the Sacraments--to say "Amen" and receive the Eucharist, or be absolved of sin and strengthened through Reconciliation—the desire to want to live chastely is required; as it is of all of us. What would motivate college-aged homosexuals to want to live chastely when the rest of society says they don't have to?

- ...a profound personal relationship with Jesus
- ...a deep reverence for the beauty of human sexuality

- ...an understanding of the nature of true sacrificial love
- ...an uncommon self-mastery
- ...a willingness to forgo marriage and children for a higher ideal
- ...an ability to see this life with the perspective of eternity; that "this slight momentary affliction is preparing us for an eternal weight of glory beyond all measure" (2 Corinthians 4:17)

All of the young people profiled once embraced the Catholicism they now shun, claiming that those principles are irreconcilable with a homosexual's nature. The church acknowledges their difficulty: "The number of men and women who have deep-seated homosexual tendencies is not negligible...These persons are called to fulfill God's will in their lives and, if they are Christians, to unite to the sacrifice of the Lord's Cross the difficulties they may encounter from their condition" (CCC 2358).

A psychologist,[52] who has seen same-sex attracted young adults, postulates that society does not provide these emerging adults with a language or conceptualization of love that is not sexual. "Many of the students I see are looking for connection and relationship but the only example of connection they see is sexual." Ryan, Jason,

---

52 This psychologist declined to be identified so as to protect her professional relationships with clients.

and Dave have, in fact, claimed at different times that emotional intimacy, not the act itself, drives them to seek the company of other gay men. "Much of my therapy focuses on what it means to be human and seen as a subject not an object, what embedded meaning their bodies have (as explained in *Theology of the Body*) and how they can connect to others in a deep, significant, and nonsexual way. Regardless of gender, sex, and sexuality, we have a very confused generation," the therapist concluded.

MOTHERS OF SORROW

Second only to the emotional turmoil felt by these same-sex attracted young people is the sorrow of their families… more specifically, their mothers. Ironically, their mothers draw strength from the very faith their children have forsaken. Yet, by the way that these mothers courageously share their stories we can see that their cross, too, is very heavy.

The Early Years:

Ryan's mom: Ryan was very different from his brothers— much more talkative and social. All through grade school and high school he struggled with anxiety and I think the anxiety was caused by the slow realization that he was gay. I remember crying myself to sleep on occasion worrying about it from the time he was ten years old.

Sally's mom: I was older when I had Sally and she was a little miracle. We dressed her in pink gingham and raised her as a little girl, but she struggled from the beginning. Was it environmental pollutants? A chromosomal disorder? My late age? Chemicals in the food supply...I don't know...she grew up chubby too? Maybe that had something to do with it? Urgh...I don't know...I don't think I realized how much influence I could have had.

Jason's mom: Jason has never told us he is gay, but ... he was really depressed one night when he was young, sitting in his bedroom looking at his computer and I went in and knelt next to him. He said "Mom I am just not going to be the kind of boy you want me to be." We both cried. I understood what we were dealing with.

Dave's mom: I would have told you when Dave was about three or four that there was something different about him. A couple of times over the years I asked him if he thought he might be gay and he denied it and got very defensive. Neither his siblings nor my husband and I were surprised when he came to terms with it.

For their physical health:
Ryan's Mom: I've read about what it can be like among gay men and I worry that Ryan will get caught up in drugs, or in a bad social scene, or in a hookup gone wrong and could literally die. He had one really scary experience which he told us about. I know he is smarter than he used to be, but I still worry...

Dave's mom: Dave's psychiatrist pointed out that he's not doing what other men like him are doing: drugs, pornography, self-harm, trolling the bars, promiscuity... Dave chose to go to a Catholic college and now he is living at home, surrounded by people with family values. These are safety nets he has set up for himself, whether he recognizes it or not. I have talked to him about being safe, safe, safe. I've been really open with him about his drinking and his overall health. He scared us with talk of suicide twice, but I think he's outgrown that and now he seems to be in a good place. Dave talks to a psychiatrist every six weeks and that schedule works for him. The older he gets the more comfortable he is.

Sally's mom: In college, she went on antidepressants, became suicidal and checked herself into the psychiatric ward. Her friends were there for her and visited. She rallied, but when her LGBTQ friends graduated, Sally followed them without finishing school.

For their future:

Ryan's mom: When Ryan finally told us, my overwhelming thought was, "Whew, now maybe some emotional healing can begin." But it's still very difficult for everyone. He really wants a long-term committed relationship—a life companion—and I want that for him too. When he comes home, he sees the grandkids running around, and his married siblings go off to their rooms two-by-two. I wonder if it's hard for Ryan...But I believe that his way would not make him happy in the long run. He disagrees with me, of course.

Jason's mom: Jason just loves kids and I want that for him...children, his own progeny. What a great source of joy and satisfaction children are, especially as you age. I worry about loneliness...He may be very lonely one day...

Sally's mom: Sally is happy with her friends, still studying...she has many piercings and tattoos and she thinks they make her look beautiful! I just don't get it...but we're friends now. I keep in touch through Facebook and text her a couple times a week. I pray about it, and I think she will be fine, really just fine.

Dave's mom: Life is just easier when you're heterosexual. I know Dave asks, "why me," because his other siblings are straight. For now, he has no interest in getting married. But I would like him to be in a relationship because I think the alternative is very lonely and pretty miserable.

For their faith:

Ryan's mom: I knew he had suffered emotionally for years, and that he was mad at God but it all became very clear when Ryan told us he was gay. We have talked very honestly about the faith and he told me one time, "I tried Catholicism. I prayed so hard when I was younger, and it didn't work out." He really did try to pray it all away. He says now, fifteen years later, that he finally feels free of the constraints Catholicism has put on him all these years and he is happy with his life.

Jason's mom: My husband is in complete denial, but I know...and it's the biggest sword in my side. Jason is at the top of my prayer list...I say every novena for him....I don't pray for anything else as fervently as for this. I have hope he will change. I don't know what I would have done differently...I just don't know...We are told it does not bring you salvation, so how can I accept it when I know it's not good for him? My other kids know, I think. But my husband would never accept it, and so I just keep praying.

Sally: When I talk to my daughter about religion and the church she tells me, "I love Jesus, but His church does not like me." In a book she read by Scott Hahn in high school, she crossed out "Marriage was made by God," and wrote in, "Marriage is a man-made construct." She does not practice her faith, yet when I told her about one of my troubles the other day, she said, "Oh Mom, I'm going to light a candle for you." I thought that was sweet. She is a good person.

Dave's mom: In high school, Dave became very religious, going to daily Mass and weekly confession. He told me later that he had been praying that he wouldn't be gay. When God didn't make Dave straight, he gave up on God. I pray every day that he comes back and I think it might be years...and not to the Catholic church. He just feels that the Catholic church doesn't have a place for him. I have given up on the idea that he'll ever become Catholic, but I hope he finds a Christian church community so that he can have Christ in his life.

MAKING BURDENS LIGHT

As fellow Christians and imitators of Jesus Christ, we are called to welcome same-sex attracted people of good will into our lives and our pews. According to the Catechism, "They must be accepted with respect, compassion, and sensitivity. Every sign of unjust discrimination in their regard should be avoided" (CCC 2358). Yet, a 2013 Pew Research Center survey found that 79 percent of LGBTQ adults who practice a faith see the Catholic church as unfriendly. Three-in-ten LGBTQ said they personally were made to feel unwelcome in a religious organization.[53]

Eve Tushnet, a Catholic gay author, describes the benefits of a church with doors wide open to same-sex attracted individuals:

> One of the parish communities in which I've served a lot of time is my church's ministry to gay and lesbian Catholics and our families and friends. This ministry is not the easiest one to work with. We try to "meet people where they are." We don't require you to have a position on the Church's teachings before you attend. That means

---

53 Caryle Murphy, "Lesbian Gay and Bisexual Americans Differ from General Public in their Religious Affiliations," *Pew Research Center,* May 26, 2015, accessed March 10, 2017, http://www.pewresearch.org/fact-tank/2015/05/26/lesbian-gay-and-bisexual-americans-differ-from-general-public-in-their-religious-affiliations.

meetings can sometimes feel like trying to herd
not just cats, but cats plus dogs plus ferrets plus
that one person who's gotta be a badger. But it also
means that people who always thought celibacy
destroyed the soul can get to know people whose
souls are nurtured by fidelity to Church teachings.
It means that people who might be antagonists if
the subject were gay marriage can come together
to reassure a mother whose son just came out to
her—who is choking back tears as she asks what
she did wrong and mourning because she believes
her son is doomed to misery in both this life and
the next. I've seen this solidarity and it's one of the
most powerful things you can imagine.[54]

By drawing strength from Christ, same-sex attracted men
and women may find the courage to live celibate, fruitful
Christian lives. Where better to meet Christ than in our
churches, among our families, in our Catholic communi-
ties? Does this make you uncomfortable? Do you wonder
how parish life would change? What kinds of conversations would happen at the dinner table? "You can't be
talking about those radical agenda-driven gays, can you?
Invite *them* to my house?" Ryan's mom thought that way...

---

54 Eve Tushnet, *Gay and Catholic: Accepting My Sexuality, Finding Community,
Living My Faith* (Notre Dame, IN: Ave Maria Press, 2014), 141-142.

Ryan asked one summer day if he could have a big party to celebrate his graduation and new job. He wanted to invite the extended family, his grade school and high school friends and his new gay friends, some of whom he warned were nontraditional. "I was conflicted," said Ryan's mom, "because I didn't want to seem to be normalizing the gay lifestyle, and, honestly, I worried about what my family would say." She and her husband prayed about it and decided to go ahead with the party. "I wasn't comfortable when a group of colorfully dressed men rounded the corner to mingle with the family but everyone handled it better than I seemed to," said Ryan's mom. "Under my breath, I quietly asked the Lord to be present, and then I gave it all over to Him. Thinking back on it, I've come to understand that Christ is the one who does the heavy lifting when it comes to conversion," she said. "All we had to do that day was offer hospitality and love the people Christ put in front of us."

Speaking in *The Joy of Love* about the family's obligation to evangelize, Pope Francis invites us to reach out to others without compromising our convictions in imitation of Jesus Christ.

We know that Jesus himself ate and drank with sinners (cf. Mark 2:16; Matthew 11:19), conversed with a Samaritan woman (cf. John 4:7-26), received Nicodemus by night (cf. John 3:1-21), allowed his feet to be anointed by a prostitute (cf. Luke

7:36-50) and did not hesitate to lay his hands on those who were sick (cf. Mark 1:40-45; 7:33). The same was true of his apostles, who did not look down on others, or cluster together in small and elite groups, cut off from the life of their people. Although the authorities harassed them, they nonetheless enjoyed the favor "of all the people" (Acts 2:47; cf. 4:21, 33; 5:13).[55]

College-aged men and women with same-sex attraction are at the peak of their physical sexual development, pummeled like everyone else by pornography, and affirmed in their same-sex attraction by most of their peers. They need our unconditional love—a love that doesn't compromise truth, but reaches out, invites, welcomes, and invests in the lives of our Christian brothers and sisters. "If one member suffers, all suffer together with it..." (1 Corinthians 12:26).

For whom are you called to be the face of Christ?

---

55 Pope Francis, *The Joy of Love: On Love in the Family* (Erlanger, KY: Beacon Publishing, 2015), 217.

Prayer

Heavenly Father, you are a wise and loving Father of *all* of us. Your care and concern for each soul You've created is profound and unchanging. You weep with those emotionally, physically, or spiritually hurt by same-sex attraction and you accompany those suffering the consequences.

Help us comprehend the beauty of chastity. Raise up heroes in our culture to testify to the sanctity of chaste marriage, chaste celibacy and chaste single living. Show us, Lord, how to please you with our sexuality.

Please bless my child _____ and all those in college with him/her. Protect all those on college campuses from sexual sin.

We ask for all these graces through the intercession of your Blessed Mother, Virgin and Queen, Mary most Pure.

Questions for Reflection:

What is my immediate emotional response to homosexuality? Anger? Fear? Curiosity? Numbness? Never thought about it? I will write down at least three of my reactions. I will discuss my thoughts with the small group, or write a prayer asking for a deeper enlightenment.

Considering the relationships I have with those who are gay in my community, at work, or in another circle of influence, how well do I radiate the love of Christ to them?

Prayer Intentions:

Answered Prayers:

Prayer Practice: The next time I am in a crowd of any size, I will scan the faces and make eye contact with someone I might not have otherwise noticed. I will offer him/her the smile of Christ, following the advice of Saint John of the Cross, "Where there is no love, put love, and there will be love."[56]

---

56   Letter from Saint John of the Cross to Madre María de la Encarnación, discalced Carmelite, July 6, 1591, Segovia, Spain.

Lord, how can I love you more today than I did yesterday?

And the Pharisees and the scribes were grumbling and saying, "This fellow welcomes sinners and eats with them." Luke 15:2

Lord, how can I love you more today than I did yesterday?

For you were called to freedom, brothers and sisters, only do not use your freedom as an opportunity for self-indulgence, but through love become slaves to one another. For the whole law is summed up in a single commandment, "You shall love your neighbor as yourself." Galatians 5:13-14

Lord, how can I love you more today than I did yesterday?

Jesus replied, "Who is my mother, and who are my brothers?"
Matthew 12:48

Lord, how can I love you more today than I did yesterday?

Whoever serves me must follow me, and where I am, there will my servant be also. Whoever serves me, the Father will honor. John 12:26

CHAPTER 11

MOM-TO-MOM ADVICE

"YOU'RE A SAINT," we commonly remark to the stranger who lifts a heavy bag into the overhead bin on a plane, or the store clerk who finds just the right size on the sale rack. Yet, that casual turn of phrase has more gravitas than we may realize. We are, in fact, surrounded by saints...in-the-making. Looking for the wisest, holiest, most reliable advice for raising children who want to live their Catholic faith brought me into touch with many saints-in-the making: mothers of college-aged young adults with dynamic, active, faithful lives, marked by a naturalness and authenticity with which they live out their personal relationship with Jesus Christ. In a beautiful spirit of humility and magnanimity, they offer some advice for helping young adults live their Catholic faith. I hope, as we wind up this time together, that you find inspiration from the women who share below their varied perspectives, their words of wisdom, and, perhaps most importantly, their humble unassuming approach to raising faith-filled children.[57] Read, however, with the following caveat: Parents feed, clothe, shelter, kiss and hug, instruct, guide, advise, educate, financially support, and so on....but "success" is the Lord's.

GETTING TO MASS

- *When we do the college tour, I make a point of finding the Catholic student center. I walk them there so they won't have to find out where it is on their own. I introduce myself to the person in charge. Then I take my child to the chapel. I tell him or her, "This is where you come for some quiet. No one will ever bother you in here."*

- *My daughter called freshman year to say she was having trouble making good friends. I encouraged her to go to Mass, even daily Mass, because she would be very likely to find nice people there! I don't know if she actually went to daily Mass but she did go on Sundays and she met some good friends before the year was over.*

- *I always found the church to be one of the few places on campus where I could find some quiet time. I can't say I prayed very well there but I used to stop in often and just sit in a pew. When my kids call from college saying they're overwhelmed, sometimes I suggest*

---

57 As with all of the women who shared their stories with me for this book series, these too were interviewed under the condition of anonymity. Rather than create names for each, I have left them unattributed.

that they go sit in the chapel and I tell them about my experience.

- Once in a while, I pull the "Mom Card." This past Christmas season was the first time everyone was home for months. That first night, I texted them all and said, "Please, please let's all go to 9 a.m. Mass together tomorrow morning. That means my car will leaving at 8:45 a.m. You don't have to go. I am just inviting you." Even though it was a Tuesday daily Mass, they all got out of bed and hopped into the car. Afterwards, we went to Dunkin Donuts and they joked, saying that, if they'd known they'd get doughnuts, they'd go to Mass every day.

- We have always gone to Mass as a family, so when the kids come back from school, it's natural that they come with us on Sunday to Mass.

- I always make it a point to be familiar with the Mass times on campus, so I can offer it up to my children in the form of a conversation...always a soft sell and just enough to give direction.

- After Confirmation in high school, it became increasingly difficult to get my daughter to go to church. My husband and I had divorced. He had never been much of a church goer and unfortunately she was following in his footsteps. "Why do I have to go? I pray in my own way. I'm still a good person." The litany of reasons were endless. It was exhausting—explaining, cajoling, threatening, dragging, begging her to come with me. Sometimes *it worked, mostly it didn't. I blamed myself on so many levels and this was absolutely not the way my family was when I was growing up. Fast forward to college and not much has changed. She has never once gone to Mass in college. It doesn't help that she's in a huge secular university in a big city. I tried linking her with the Neumann Society, suggesting she bring up going to Mass at certain holidays as a way to find out what roommates/classmates might be interested. She actually went so far as to find a church, ask a friend...but didn't end up attending. Now on her internship in a major city, alone, afraid, she actually found her way to a major cathedral...Small steps...I know she prays. I know she thinks about it. I know she believes. It's going to be on her own schedule and when the call from God hits her on the head. I'm sure of it. So I pray that she accepts prayer as part of her life. She's stubborn. So was I. She's searching. I still am. My daughter, myself. He is with us. I believe...He's with her...she just doesn't know it yet.*

GOING TO CONFESSION

- *We go to Sunday Mass where they offer Confession before Mass. When my kids are home from school, they almost always take advantage of the availability of Confession right before Mass starts.*

- *I don't have that conversation with my college kids about when they last went to Confession, but when we are together before Mass and I see a priest in the Confessional, I point it out and they usually get in line.*
- *When I know that Confessions are being offered and they're home, I sometimes text them, more as an informational thing, but they go.*
- *Our family has a habit of attending a parish-wide reconciliation service on the Sundays before Christmas and Easter. Soft music is played, there is a short service where the Act of Contrition is said as a group, and then the priests are introduced. It's the least "in your face" way to go to confession I've ever seen!*

KEEPING THE FAITH THROUGH SERVICE

- *My husband took our sons on a mission trip to El Salvador and it was a life-changing experience for all of them. They came back right before Christmas saying, "We are so blessed. We live such a luxurious lifestyle. These people have nothing." The group had brought soccer equipment to hand out, but they also said the rosary, prayed and sang with the families there. My husband had never experienced that they could share their faith with others as well as have the fun that comes with soccer.*

- *I asked my daughter to consider teaching religious education at the parish she attended at college, knowing that service would keep her looking outward. She decided, instead, to babysit for the morning Masses, making $15 an hour. Then she went to Mass in the evening. I liked that her "job" kept her at Church.*

- *After going to Ash Wednesday service, my daughter, with her Catholic friends, took bags of clothes they collected from their closets and distributed them to the homeless downtown.*

- *My daughter got involved in a program at college that does community service. It wasn't particularly spiritual, but I believe that the experiences she had in the inner city helped her to appreciate her faith and her many blessings.*

SPIRITUAL ACCOMPANIMENT

- *All the while my kids were growing up my husband and I went monthly to spiritual direction as part of our regular routine. When my daughter was in high school, she had spiritual direction as part of a retreat and she sometimes got extended guidance during Confession at her high school. When she went to college, she sought out a lay consecrated woman who lived nearby and came to campus once a month to see her. I don't know what they*

    talked about but I'm convinced that's what helped her
    keep her faith through college.

- *When anything big happened at college, the kids would call and ask for our prayers. "Pray for my test, please," or "Pray for this big presentation." They always knew we would. And my husband and I tell them often that we pray for them every day.*

- *I tell them I am praying for them, especially when they are experiencing difficulties or having exams. They laugh that "prayer" is Mom's answer to everything. I just raise my eyebrows, smile and shrug. I tell them to just keep seeking the Truth.*

ALL IN THE FAMILY

- *I make a point to appreciate when we're all together— so much so that the kids tease me about it. But I think it's important to relish and call attention to those times, which become rarer and rarer as they're growing into adulthood, that we can be together and enjoy each other's company.*

- *We are a big family, and there are lots of weddings and funerals. Every time we go to a funeral we are all in the same car, so I start the Divine Mercy Chaplet...and they all pray it with me. On the way to a wedding we pray for the bride and groom and for their future. I try to pray like that out loud just in certain moments so that they learn how to pray, and can roll up their sleeves and make good use of their faith.*

- *My older daughter asked me why I suggest we give up something every Lent as a family. "Isn't it supposed to be about loving more, not being told what to do," one asked? I reminded her that we are a family. We eat together, do fun things together, pray together, and sometimes we sacrifice together. We are asking God to bless us as a family, and so we make a "family sacrifice." She wasn't convinced but she acquiesced. I hope she is learning something about the importance of unity in the family.*

- *I have to remind myself that they are good, loving kids, who seem to have absorbed and practice many of the basic tenets of faith that we tried to instill in them, and that God is in charge of this. And my husband reminds me that they have to make their faith their own—by this age they should be questioning and coming to an understanding of what they believe. Instead of stressing about my children's faith, which I cannot force upon them, I have found that perhaps I need to do a little soul searching myself and work on developing my faith...and become more dependent on [God.]*

As Praying College Moms know, the most important parenting tool God gives us is our capacity to pray. When we pray, we avail ourselves of the gifts of the Holy Spirit: wisdom, understanding, counsel, fortitude, knowledge, piety, and fear of the Lord (wonder). There are no better parenting skills!

Remembering that we are beloved daughters of Our Heavenly Father, we intercede for our children with child-like trust and confidence, accomplishing the ultimate good for our children. When we wait for prayers to be answered, we can draw consolation from our friend, Saint Tèresé of Lisieux, who captures the earnest desire of a mother for the salvation of her children in these words she wrote about the souls for whom she prays:

> O Jesus, it is not even necessary to say: "When drawing me, draw the souls whom I love!" ... All the souls whom [the soul] loves follow in her train; this is done without constraint, without effort. It is a natural consequence of her attraction for You.
>
> Just as a torrent, throwing itself with impetu-osity into the ocean drags, after it everything it encounters in its passage, in the same way, O Jesus, the soul who plunges into the shoreless ocean of your love draws with her all the treasures she pos-sesses...I have no other treasures than the souls it has pleased You to unite to mine."[58]

---

58 John Clarke, OCD, *Story of a Soul: The Autobiography of Térèsè of Lisieux*, 3rd ed. (Washington, DC: ICS Publications, 1996), 254.

It is my personal prayer that the irresistible truth of our spiritual daughterhood motivates you to pray continually and to ever-deepen your personal relationship with God, for your personal benefit, for the sake of your college-aged young adults, and for all of us who are raised up by the prayers of other saints-in-the-making!

God's fatherhood in regard to us is the deepest reality there is, the richest and most inexpressible, an inconceivable abyss of life and mercy. There is no greater source of happiness than being a son or daughter, living in the moment of this fatherhood, receiving oneself and receiving everything from God's goodness and generosity; confidently expecting everything, at every moment of our lives from God's gift."[59]

---

59 Fr. Jacque Philippe, *Thirsting for Prayer* (New Rochelle, NY: Scepter Publishers, 2014), 25.

A Closing Prayer

Dearest Father in Heaven,

You delight in me, as a mother delights in the first smiles of her infant child. Praise Your Eternal Parenthood, Heavenly Father.

You nourish me with the Eucharist, as a mother tenderly feeds her infant. Praise Your eternal provision, Heavenly Father.

You graciously heal my woundedness through the Sacrament of Reconciliation, as a mother kisses wet cheeks and dries the tears of her toddler. Praise Your eternal benevolence, Heavenly Father.

When I'm fearful and anxious, You offer me "peace that surpasses all understanding" (Philippians 4:7), a peace much more transcendent than an earthly mother can give to her child. I praise You Father, giver of every good gift.

With awe and reverence, I praise you for Your Holy Spirit, and for the gift of your Son, Jesus Christ, my savior and redeemer, and His Mother Mary who has become my mother. We are family, Heavenly Father.

Father, I thank You for the gift of my children and I ask You most solemnly for the grace to be the best possible parent in imitation of You. Knowing that "without You I can do nothing" (John 15:4) I entrust my children to Your care, confident that You will guide us all to fulfill Your will on our earthly journey, and reunite us one day with You in heaven.

Questions for Reflection:

Knowing that prayer is a powerful aid to my children, how do I pray? Am I riddled with anxiety? Unsure of what to pray for? Highly distracted? Doubting that prayer makes a difference and, therefore, praying infrequently or not at all? Discuss or journal about how embracing the truth about our spiritual daughterhood can combat these and other obstacles to prayer.

Prayer Intentions:

Answered Prayers:

Prayer Practice:
I will prayerfully evaluate my spiritual progress this past year, thanking God for all the good, and resolving, with God's grace, to improve in one area of weakness as discerned in prayer.

APPENDIX 1

ABOUT PRAYING COLLEGE MOMS

PRAYING COLLEGE MOMS was founded on the belief that mothers have a unique opportunity to lift our children to the Lord in prayer and entrust them to His care. Our network of praying moms is founded on the following six pillars of our faith:

- We follow the example of the Holy Mother to pray for our child(ren).
- We trust God to have a bigger, better plan for our children than any of us might envision for them.
- We believe in the power of prayer to change the lives of our students as they are away from our care.
- We cede control of our children's lives to the Father and enter into intercessory prayer on their behalf.
- We pledge support, mentorship, guidance and prayer to our fellow mothers of college-aged children and those transitioning from having a high school senior to a college freshman.

- We bless our children with regular care packages with a Catholic twist to bolster their emotional and spiritual health.

WHO WE ARE:

As a new small-faith community group, Praying College Moms offers a place for moms to share what they are praying for—and how—and offers support and advice as needed. Every college-age student's experience takes them to new levels of questions and maturity. Sometimes college-age students don't want help navigating these challenges, but moms know their kids still need the basics: love and understanding! Talking through one student's darkness and another student's light, our group's focus is on hope, optimism, and care. These moms feast on prayer and fast from worry—and help each other along the way!

Laurel Howanitz, the mother of four children, founded the original group at Saint Mark's in Fall 2012. "I began this group to help moms with college age kids forge a camaraderie with other college moms through Christian fellowship. We used to live in Knoxville, Tennessee, and our parish there had a similar group that really helped me a lot when my older children went off to college."

Praying College Moms groups typically meet once a month for approximately one and a half hours. The group facilitator makes introductions and opens the meeting with prayer. She may solicit prayer intentions from the group. After the opening prayer, the leader initiates a discussion based on the theme suggested by a chapter of the book. She may read the "Questions for Reflection" and/ or highlight some lines from the chapter she feels are thought provoking. To close the meeting, the leader prays aloud or invites another team member to do so.

Periodically, the group meets to prepare care packages, say the rosary, or provide some service for the parish, all at the discretion of the group members. PCM groups may go on hiatus during the summer months. Once a month allows for busy moms to fit it in their schedule without being overwhelmed. The chemistry and easy flow of our groups make it so easy to share problems, ideas and joys! It is a great sounding board.

The care packages are a way for parents and families to engage in supporting their college children around the country. Many parents don't think to make care packages, and our care package program makes it easy to send your child a token of your love on a regular basis. The groups gather an enjoyable and fun variety of items for the boxes, and the positive student feedback confirms that our children love receiving their goodies.

The shared experiences of mothers going through the empty-nest college years instills trust in group members. If a situation arises with our college age child, we trust that we can confidentially share our concerns in our group and receive helpful input and insights from other mothers. Some come to gain support as they guide their kids on their journey of discovery and maturation, from a spiritual foundation. We also recognize the power of a group praying together with one voice as a vital force in our lives. This power helps us cede control and trust that all is in God's hands.

We believe this prayer helps the students see God's role in planning and directing their lives more to God as they leave the nest. Our fervent hope is that our students will learn to recognize that any peace and joy they experience is from God. It is also an indication that they are making the "right" choices in their curriculum choices, career planning, relationships, and general good health and well-being. In a time when their rational mind still isn't fully formed, they need to learn to trust in God *and* seek the advice of professionals to make their decisions. We all know the result when they learn only from their peers!

The moms pray hard for all college-age young adults. Most pray daily for all the college age students in their parish, that they may hear and recognize God at work in their lives, keep their moral integrity, achieve their academic goals, experience intellectual growth and academic success, make good interpersonal choices, maintain good health and sleeping routines, and daily inspire and help those in need around them.

APPENDIX 2

HOW TO USE THIS BOOK IN PCM SMALL GROUPS

...And So We Pray 2 was written to help individuals or women meeting in small groups to draw peace and consolation from God as children go off to college.

PCM small groups support each other in prayer and friendship, meeting during the school year to explore themes from one chapter each month.

The first chapter lays the groundwork for the rest of the book, emphasizing the importance of a filial relationship with God and constancy in prayer. Small-Group leaders may want to spend more time with this material, referring to it repeatedly, to reinforce the importance of fidelity to prayer and love of God the Father.

The Praying College Moms community is a welcoming, Christian environment where every member of a small group can share with confidence their inner most concerns, assured of confidentiality and compassion on the part of the other members. Through mutual support, prayer, and friendship, the group is meant to be a pillar of strength and an indispensable resource for women at this stage in life.

A Sample Meeting (approximately seventy-five to ninety minutes)

- Opening prayer and welcome—fifteen minutes
- Chapter review—PCM's review one chapter during each monthly meeting. Share thoughts or comments from the chapter, addressing any questions that arise—thirty minutes
- Discussion of questions—Read aloud the Questions for Reflection and discuss—fifteen minutes
- Review the Prayer Practice—Is this doable during the next month? Why or why not? —five minutes
- Closing prayers sharing intentions—ten minutes

Other optional elements:

- Care Package planning and/or assembly (see the website for details)
- Extended prayer/monthly rosary

For more information, go to www.prayingcollegemoms.org. Individuals are also very welcome to contact the author through that website or www.andsowepray.com to share their own stories with the author.

APPENDIX 3

TEN WEEKS TO FINDING JOY

Week 1] I will humble myself—Joy is a gift and can't be manufactured. It is a fruit of the Holy Spirit. (CCC 1832) I open my heart to acknowledge my weaknesses and neediness and ask You, Lord, for the gift of Joy.

Week 2] I make a covenant with You, Lord. I commit wholeheartedly to living more joyfully by growing in knowledge and love of you by being faithful to ten to fifteen minutes of morning prayer, even on weekends and during vacations.

Week 3] I will stop complaining…out loud. It's impossible to change a habit of negative thought overnight but I will begin by catching the ones that escape through my lips. I will listen to myself and resolve to silence criticism, pessimistic comments, or little or big complaints. Instead, I will exchange those thoughts for "praise You, Lord, in all circumstances." It may not feel natural at first, but that's OK. With Your grace, I will succeed in changing my negative thought patterns.

Week 4] I will find more time for silence by turning off the radio in the car…taking the dog for a walk alone…deleting social media apps. I will use these new-found moments to seek Your presence and appreciate my surroundings.

Week 5] I will be fully present to the other. I will give eye contact, affirmation and full attention to the person in front of me at each moment of my day. I will not look to see who else is around, anticipate my next comment, or wish their presence away.

Week 6] I will do one thing at a time. When I'm driving, I'll ignore the cellphone. When I'm eating, I won't read the paper. I will focus on the task at hand, do my best work, and finish it before I move on to the next thing.

Week 7] I will cultivate an attitude of gratitude. Not everyone is born an optimist, but everyone has the capacity to change thought patterns, so I will fill my mind with gratitude for the people in my life, with appreciation for my creature comforts, with love of nature. I will celebrate the blessings in life! I will savor the glass of wine, steep in the bubble bath, rejoice with others in their accomplishments, and relish my own. I will live the virtue of Eutrapelia-- a playfulness that refreshes the soul.... I thank You, God, for these things. I will write them down in a gratitude journal.

Week 8] I will examine my friendships. Am I a good friend? Loyal, cheerful, steadfast? I resolve to improve wherever necessary. Do I have good friends? "Whoever walks with the wise becomes wise, but the companion of fools suffers harm"(Proverbs 13:20). I will pray, asking You for good friends and to be a better friend.

Week 9] I will observe and reflect. With more silence in my life and a regular habit of prayer, I am starting to recognize patterns in my behavior. I will appreciate my God-given talents. This is not a lack of humility: I'm practicing humility by recognizing in truth who I am before You, Lord. I will take my weaknesses and faults to You in the Sacrament of Reconciliation to be healed and strengthened.

Week 10] I will look for opportunities to share my joy with others, especially those less fortunate. Present me, Lord, with the "poor" You wish for me to serve...the poor in temporal gifts and those poor in spirit.

APPENDIX 4

WHAT IS MORTAL SIN?

EXCERPTS FROM THE Catechism of the Catholic Church

1855 *Mortal sin* destroys charity in the heart of man by a grave violation of God's law; it turns man away from God, who is his ultimate end and his beatitude, by preferring an inferior good to him.

Venial sin allows charity to subsist, even though it offends and wounds it.

1856 Mortal sin, by attacking the vital principle within us - that is, charity - necessitates a new initiative of God's mercy and a conversion of heart which is normally accomplished within the setting of the sacrament of reconciliation:

When the will sets itself upon something that is of its nature incompatible with the charity that orients man toward his ultimate end, then the sin is mortal by its very object . . . whether it contradicts the love of God, such as blasphemy or perjury, or the love of neighbor, such as homicide or adultery. . . . But when the sinner's will is set upon something that of its nature involves a disorder, but is not opposed to the love of God and neighbor, such as thoughtless chatter or immoderate laughter and the like, such sins are venial.[130]

1857 For a *sin* to be *mortal*, three conditions must together be met: "Mortal sin is sin whose object is grave matter and which is also committed with full knowledge and deliberate consent."[131]

1858 *Grave matter* is specified by the Ten Commandments, corresponding to the answer of Jesus to the rich young man: "Do not kill, Do not commit adultery, Do not steal, Do not bear false witness, Do not defraud, Honor your father and your mother."[132] The gravity of sins is more or less great: murder is graver than theft. One must also take into account who is wronged: violence against parents is in itself graver than violence against a stranger.

1859 Mortal sin requires *full knowledge* and *complete consent*. It presupposes knowledge of the sinful character of the act, of its opposition to God's law. It also implies a consent sufficiently deliberate to be a personal choice. Feigned ignorance and hardness of heart[133] do not diminish, but rather increase, the voluntary character of a sin.

1860 *Unintentional ignorance* can diminish or even remove the imputability of a grave offense. But no one is deemed to be ignorant of the principles of the moral law, which are written in the conscience of every man. The promptings of feelings and passions can also diminish the voluntary and free character of the offense, as can external pressures or pathological disorders. Sin committed through malice, by deliberate choice of evil, is the gravest.

1861 Mortal sin is a radical possibility of human freedom, as is love itself. It results in the loss of charity and the privation of sanctifying grace, that is, of the state of grace. If it is not redeemed by repentance and God's forgiveness, it causes exclusion from Christ's kingdom and the eternal death of hell, for our freedom has the power to make choices for ever, with no turning back. However, although we can judge that an act is in itself a grave offense, we must entrust judgment of persons to the justice and mercy of God.

ABOUT THE AUTHOR

MARIBETH HARPER BEGAN as a professional writer 35 years ago, working in Washington DC for a national telecommunications publishing house. More recently, she has co-chaired the Something Greater Ministry, (somethinggreater.net) for which she edits and writes; edited for a national women's bible study program, Walking with Purpose (walkingwithpurpose.com); and provided website development and consulting for a variety of mission-based clients. She spent six years working with adolescent girls in Catholic faith formation programs and eight years as the co-chair and business manager of the largest fashion show on the East coast – Pure Fashion, which promotes modesty among high school girls. She speaks to women at retreats and bible studies on topics of prayer and family life. She has four grown children, four grand-children, and lives in Maryland with her husband of 33 years, Denis.

Maribeth has authored two books for the Praying College Moms group: *...And So We Pray* and *...And So We Pray 2*. It is her ardent wish that the stories shared by women of faith in these books will help all women with college-aged young adults—individuals and Praying College Moms—to grow in their relationship with God through prayer, and thereby provide the most effective and fruitful help to their children and their families.

www.andsowepray.com

47754878R00119

Made in the USA
Middletown, DE
01 September 2017